Málaga &
Costa del Sol

Andy Symington

Credits

Footprint credits
Editor: Sophie Jones
Production and layout: Emma Bryers
Maps: Kevin Feeney

Publisher: Patrick Dawson
Managing Editor: Felicity Laughton
Advertising: Elizabeth Taylor
Sales and marketing: Kirsty Holmes

Photography credits
Front cover: Shutterstock/
Arena Photo UK
Back cover: Dreamstime/
Montserrat Fernández Tamayo

Printed in Great Britain by Alphaset,
Surbiton, Surrey

Every effort has been made to ensure
that the facts in this guidebook are
accurate. However, travellers should
still obtain advice from consulates,
airlines, etc, about travel and visa
requirements before travelling. The
authors and publishers cannot accept
responsibility for any loss, injury or
inconvenience however caused.

Publishing information
Footprint *Focus Málaga & Costa del Sol*
2nd edition
© Footprint Handbooks Ltd
February 2014

ISBN: 978 1 909268 80 7
CIP DATA: A catalogue record
for this book is available from
the British Library

® Footprint Handbooks and the
Footprint mark are a registered
trademark of Footprint Handbooks Ltd

Published by Footprint
6 Riverside Court
Lower Bristol Road
Bath BA2 3DZ, UK
T +44 (0)1225 469141
F +44 (0)1225 469461
footprinttravelguides.com

Distributed in the USA by Globe
Pequot Press, Guilford, Connecticut

Contents

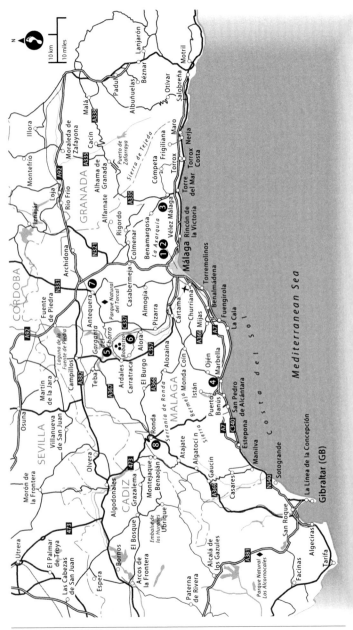

Málaga may be the smallest province in Andalucía, but it compensates with its significant population and economy, much of it based on tourism. The Costa del Sol is still pulling the crowds decades on, with a vast influx of Northern European and Spanish tourists every year, and a large expat population.

The small-time fishing villages strung along this coast are long gone, swallowed by overdevelopment, a line of beachside apartments, hotels, bars and golf courses that stretches almost unbroken the length of the province. Venture inland, however, and you will discover a more authentic Spain. Despite the rise in rural tourism, towns like Antequera, with its prehistoric dolmens, have evocative historic appeal, while more recent Moorish influence is seen throughout the region, particularly in architecture and culture.

Less than an hour away from the glitzy but notorious resort of Marbella, the ancient town of Ronda is a stunning sight, set on the El Tajo gorge, while nearby *pueblos blancos* (white villages) are timelessly preserved – and you still need Spanish to order a beer.

Inland mountain ranges include the Serranía de Ronda and the limestone block of El Torcal, with its surreal eroded shapes. Rivers have cut deep gorges, such as El Chorro, and many have been dammed to form reservoirs, such as Guadalhorce. East of Málaga is the dramatic La Axarquía and pretty white villages with unpronounceable names.

The provincial capital is vastly underrated Málaga itself, Andalucía's second largest city, which has lively nightlife, a Picasso museum, trendy shops and some of the region's best tapas bars. The town beach is actually a more attractive strip of sand than many of the gravelly offerings of the Costa del Sol.

Planning your trip

Getting to Málaga and the Costa del Sol

Málaga's busy **airport** ⓘ *T952-048844, www.aena.es or the good unofficial page www.malagaairport.eu,* is named after Pablo Picasso and handles some 12 million passengers a year. It's located 7 km west of the city centre. A taxi will cost you €20-25. The cheapest method of reaching the city centre from the airport is the Fuengirola–Málaga train, every 30 minutes from 0700 to midnight (€1.70-2.60 single). The journey takes 15 minutes. There are two Málaga stations; the final Centro-Alameda stop is more central. There are also buses between the airport and the Alameda at half-hourly intervals between 0630 and 2300.

The **bus** station is conveniently close to the main train station on Paseo de los Tilos. There are bus links with all the major Andalucían cities and beyond, including many buses along the coast in both directions. It's a 20-minute walk to the city centre from the train and bus stations or take a local bus. The train station has a high-speed *AVE* rail link to and from Madrid via Córdoba, as well as a commuter service along the coast to Fuengirola via the airport, Torremolinos and Benalmadena (see above). The line is due to be extended west to Marbella and Estepona; another branch heads north to Alhora. For other destinations in the province, travel by car or bus tends to be cheaper and more reliable.
➤ *See Transport, page 30.*

Tourist information
The main **regional tourist office** ⓘ *T952-308911, Mon-Fri 0900-1930, Sat and Sun 0930-1500, otmalaga@andalucia.org,* is at Pasaje Chinitas 4. The **municipal tourist office** ⓘ *Pl de la Marina, T952-926020, www.malagaturismo.com, daily 0900-1800 (2000 Apr-Oct),* is between the port and the centre. This can provide you with a free audio guide to the city, plus various thematic self-guided walking tours. There are also smaller tourist offices at the airport and bus station, plus several information kiosks in the centre.

Where to stay in Málaga and the Costa del Sol

The standard of accommodation in Andalucía is very high; even the most modest of *pensiones* is usually very clean and respectable. *Alojamientos* (places to stay) are divided into two main categories; the distinctions between them are in an arcane series of regulations devised by the government. *Hoteles*

Don't miss...

(marked H or HR) are graded from one to five stars and occupy their own building, which distinguishes them from many *hostales* (Hs or HsR), which go from one to two stars. The *hostal* category includes *pensiones*, the standard budget option, typically family-run and occupying a floor of an apartment building. The standard for the price paid is normally excellent, and they're nearly all spotless. Spanish traditions of hospitality are alive and well; even the simplest of *pensiones* will provide a towel and soap, and check-out time is almost uniformly a very civilized midday.

A great number of Spanish hotels are well equipped but characterless chain business places (big players include **NH**, www.nh-hoteles.es; **Husa**, www.husa.es; **AC**, www.ac-hotels.com; **Tryp/SolMelia**, www.melia.com and **Hesperia**, www.hoteles-hesperia.es), and are often situated outside the old town. This guide has expressly minimized these in the listings, preferring to concentrate on more atmospheric options. If you're booking accommodation not listed in this guide, always be sure to check the location if that's important to you – it's easy to find yourself a 15-minute cab ride from the town you think you're going to be in.

An excellent option if you've got your own transport are the networks of rural houses, called *casas rurales*. Although these are under a different classification system, the standard is often as high as any country hotel. The best of them are traditional farmhouses or characterful village cottages. Some are available only to rent out whole (often for a minimum of three days), while others offer rooms on a nightly basis. Rates tend to be excellent compared to hotels. While many are listed in the text, there are huge numbers of them. Local tourist offices will have details of nearby *casas rurales*; there's also a complete listing for Andalucía available; you can also browse them online at www.andalucia.org. You can buy the useful *Guía de Alojamiento Rural*, published by El País/Aguilar, from most bookshops. Another resource for finding and booking rural accommodation is the website www.toprural.com.

Price codes

Where to stay

€€€€ over €170   €€€ €110-170
€€ €55-110   € under €55

Price codes refer to the cost of a standard double/twin room in high season (including VAT).

Restaurants

€€€ over €20   €€ €10-20   € under €10

Prices refer to the average cost of a main course, not including drinks.

There's a network of *albergues* (youth hostels), which are listed at www.inturjoven.com. These are all open year round and are very comfortable, though institutional and not especially cheap.

Most campsites are set up as well-equipped holiday villages for families; some are open only in summer. While the facilities are good, they get extremely busy in peak season; the social scene is lively, but sleep can be tough. Many have cabins or bungalows available, ranging from simple huts to houses with fully equipped kitchens and bathrooms. In other areas, camping, unless specifically prohibited, is a matter of common sense.

All registered accommodations charge a 10% value added tax; this is often included in the price at cheaper places and may be waived if you pay cash. If you have any problems, a last resort is to ask for the *libro de reclamaciones* (complaints book), an official document that, like stepping on cracks in the pavement, means uncertain but definitely horrible consequences for the hotel if anything is written in it. If resorting to this, be aware that you must also take a copy to the local police station for the complaint to be registered.

The rates are generally for high season (June-August on the coast). Occasionally, an area or town will have a short period when prices are hugely exaggerated; this is usually due to a festival. Low-season accommodation can be significantly cheaper; up to half in some coastal areas.

Many mid- to top-range city hotels cater for business travellers during the week and keep prices accordingly high. The flipside is that they usually have special weekend rates that can be exceptionally good value. Typically, these involve staying on the Friday and Saturday night and prebooking. Breakfast will often be thrown in gratis and the whole deal can save you more than 50% on the quoted prices. It's always worth investigating these and other offers by phoning ahead or checking the website.

The most useful websites for saving on hotel rates in Spain are www.booking.com, www.hotels.com and www.laterooms.com.

Normally only the more expensive hotels have parking, and they always charge for it, normally around €12-20 per day. Breakfast is often included in the price at small intimate hotels, but rarely at the grander places, who tend to charge a fortune for what is nothing more than bog-standard morning fare.

Food and drink in Málaga and the Costa del Sol

In no country in the world are culture and society as intimately connected with eating and drinking as in Spain, and in Andalucía, the spiritual home of tapas, this is even more the case. Spain's food and drink culture is significantly different from elsewhere in the EU.

Food ➔ *See page 101 for a glossary of food.*
Andalucían cooking is characterized by an abundance of fresh ingredients, generally consecrated with the chef's holy trinity of garlic, peppers and, of course, local olive oil.

Spaniards eat little for breakfast and, apart from in touristy places, you're unlikely to find anything beyond a *tostada* (large piece of toasted bread spread with olive oil, tomato and garlic, paté or jam) or a pastry to go with your coffee. Another common breakfast or afternoon snack are *churros*, long fried doughnuts that will either delight or disgust, and are typically dipped in cups of hot chocolate.

Lunch is most people's main meal of the day and is nearly always a filling affair with three courses. Most places open for lunch at about 1300, and stop serving food at 1500 or 1530, although at weekends this can extend. Lunchtime is the cheapest time to eat if you opt for the ubiquitous *menú del día*, usually a set three-course meal that includes wine or soft drink, typically costing €9 to €15. In these straitened economic times in Spain, restaurants are increasingly offering a *menú de noche*, a set evening meal that can be a real boon for the traveller. Dinner and/or evening tapas time is from around 2100 to midnight. It's not much fun sitting alone in a restaurant so try and adapt to the local hours; it may feel strange leaving dinner until so late, but you'll miss out on a lot of atmosphere if you don't. If a place is open for lunch at noon, or dinner at 1900, it's likely to be a tourist trap.

The great joy of eating out in Andalucía is, of course, going for tapas. This word refers to bar food, which is served in saucer-sized *tapa* portions typically costing €1.50-3. Tapas are available at lunchtime, but the classic time to eat them is in the evening. To do tapas the Andalucían way don't order more than a couple at each place, taste each others' dishes, and stay put at the bar. Locals know what the specialities of each bar are; it's worth asking, and if there's a daily special, order that. Also available are *raciones*, substantial meal-sized plates of the same fare, which also come in halves, *media raciones*. Both varieties are good for sharing. Considering these, the distinction between restaurants and tapas bars more or less disappears, as in the latter you can usually sit down at a table to order your *raciones*, effectively turning the experience into a meal.

Other types of eatery include the *chiringuito*, a beach bar open in summer and serving drinks and fresh seafood. A *freiduría* is a takeaway specializing in fried fish, while a *marisquería* is a classier type of seafood restaurant. In rural areas, look out for *ventas*, roadside eateries that often have a long history of feeding the passing muleteers with generous, hearty and cheap portions. The more cars and trucks outside, the better it will be. In cities, North African-style teahouses, *teterías*, are popular. These are great places with a range of teas and coffees, and a romantic, intimate atmosphere.

Vegetarians in Andalucía won't be spoiled for choice, but at least what there is tends to be good. There are few dedicated vegetarian restaurants and many restaurants won't have a vegetarian main course on offer, although the existence of tapas, *raciones* and salads makes this less of a burden than it might be. You'll have to specify *soy vegetariano/a* (I am a vegetarian), but ask what dishes contain, as ham, fish and even chicken are often considered suitable vegetarian fare. Vegans will have a tougher time.

Typical starters you'll see on set menus include *gazpacho* (a cold summer tomato soup flavoured with garlic, olive oil and peppers; *salmorejo* is a thicker version from Córdoba), *ensalada mixta* (mixed salad based on lettuce, tomatoes, tuna and more), or paella.

Main courses will usually be either meat or fish and are almost never served with any accompaniment beyond chips or marinated peppers. Beef is common throughout; cheaper cuts predominate, but better steaks such as *solomillo* or *entrecot* are usually superbly tender. Spaniards tend to eat them rare (*poco hecho*; ask for *al punto* for medium rare or *bien hecho* for well done). Pork is also widespread; *solomillo de cerdo*, *secreto*, *pluma* and *lomo* are all tasty cuts. Animal innards are popular: *callos* (tripe), *mollejas* (sweetbreads) and *morcilla* (black pudding) are excellent, if acquired, tastes.

Seafood is the pride of Andalucía. The region is famous for its *pescaíto frito* (fried fish) which typically consists of small fry such as whitebait in batter. Shellfish include *mejillones* (mussels), *gambas* (prawns) and *coquillas* (cockles). *Calamares* (calamari), *sepia* or *choco* (cuttlefish) and *chipirones* (small squid) are common, and you'll sometimes see *pulpo* (octopus). Among the vertebrates, *sardinas* (sardines), *dorada* (gilthead bream), *rape* (monkfish) and *pez espada* (swordfish) are all usually excellent. In inland areas you can enjoy freshwater *trucha* (trout).

Signature tapas dishes vary from bar to bar and part of the delight of Andalucía comes trying regional specialities. Ubiquitous are *jamón* (cured ham; the best, *ibérico*, comes from black-footed acorn-eating porkers that roam the woods of Huelva province and Extremadura) and *queso* (usually the hard salty *manchego* from Castilla-la Mancha). *Gambas* (prawns) are usually on the tapas list; the best and priciest are from Huelva. *Adobe* is marinated fried nuggets of fish, usually dogfish.

Desserts focus on the sweet and milky. *Flan* (a sort of crème caramel) is ubiquitous; great when *casero* (home-made), but often out of a plastic tub. *Natillas* are a similar but more liquid version, while Moorish-style pastries are also specialities of some areas.

Drink

Alcoholic drinks In good Catholic fashion, wine is the blood of Spain. It's the standard accompaniment to most meals, but also features prominently in bars. *Tinto* is red (if you just order *vino* it's assumed that's what you want), *blanco* is white and rosé is *rosado*.

A well-regulated system of *denominaciones de origen* (DO), similar to the French *appelation controlée*, has lifted the quality and reputation of Spanish wines high above the party plonk status they once enjoyed. While the daddy in terms of production and popularity is still Rioja, regions such as the Ribera del Duero, Rueda, Bierzo, Jumilla, Priorat and Valdepeñas have achieved worldwide recognition. The words *crianza*, *reserva* and *gran reserva* refer to the length of the ageing process.

One of the joys of Spain, though, is the rest of the wine. Order a *menú del día* at a cheap restaurant and you'll be unceremoniously served a cheap bottle of local red. Wine snobbery can leave by the back door at this point: it may be cold, but you'll find it refreshing; it may be acidic, but once the olive-oil laden food arrives, you'll be glad of it. People add water to it if they feel like it, or *gaseosa* (lemonade) or cola (for the party drink *calimocho*).

Andalucía produces several table wines of this sort. The whites of the Condado region in eastern Huelva province and those from nearby Cádiz are simple seafood companions, while in the Alpujarra region the nut-brown *costa*, somewhere between a conventional red and a rosé, accompanies the likeably simple local fare. In the same area, Laujar de Andarax produces some tasty cheapish reds. Jaén province also has red grapes tucked between its seas of olive trees, mainly around Torreperogil near Ubeda. Bartenders throughout Andalucía tend to assume that tourists only want Rioja, so be sure to specify *vino corriente* (or *vino de la zona*) if you want to try the local stuff. As a general rule, only bars that serve food serve wine; most *pubs* and *discotecas* won't have it. Cheaper red wine is often served cold, a refreshing alternative in summer. Variations on the theme are *tinto de verano* (a summery mix of red wine and lemonade, often with fruit added) or the stronger *sangría*, which adds healthy measures of sherry and sometimes spirits to the mix. The real vinous fame of the region comes, of course, from its fortified wines; sherries and others.

Beer is mostly lager, usually reasonably strong, fairly gassy, cold and good. Sweetish Cruzcampo from Sevilla is found throughout the region; other local brews include San Miguel, named after the archangel and brewed in Málaga, and Alhambra from Granada. A *caña* or *tubo* is a glass of draught beer, while just specifying *cerveza* usually gets you a bottle, otherwise known as a *botellín*. Many people order their beer *con gas*, topped up with *gaseosa*, or order a *clara*, which is a shandy. A *jarra* is a shared jug. In some pubs, particularly those specializing in different beers, you can order *pintas* (pints).

Vermut (vermouth) is a popular pre-lunch aperitif. Many bars make their own vermouth by adding various herbs and fruits and letting it sit in barrels: this can be excellent, particularly if it's from a *solera*.

After dinner it's time for a *copa*. People relax over a whisky or a brandy, or hit the *cubatas* (mixed drinks): *gin tonic* is obvious; whisky or rum with coke are the other mainstays. Spirits are free-poured and large.

When ordering a spirit, you'll be expected to choose which brand you want; the local varieties (eg Larios gin, DYC whisky) are marginally cheaper than their imported brethren but lower in quality. The range of, particularly, gins, is extraordinary. There's always a good selection of rum (*ron*) and blended whisky available too. *Chupitos* are short drinks often served in shot-glasses; restaurants will often throw in a free digestive one (usually a herb liqueur) at the end of a meal.

Non-alcoholic drinks *Zumo* (fruit juice) is normally bottled and expensive; *mosto* (grape juice, really pre-fermented wine) is a cheaper and popular soft drink in bars. All bars serve alcohol-free beer (*cerveza sin alcohol*). *Horchata* is a summer drink, a sort of milkshake made from tiger nuts. *Agua* (water) comes *con* (with) or *sin* (without) *gas*. The tap water is totally safe to drink.

Café (coffee) is usually excellent and strong. *Solo* is black, mostly served espresso style. Order *americano* if you want a long black, *cortado* if you want a dash of milk, or *con leche* for about half milk. A *carajillo* is a coffee with brandy. *Té* (tea) is served without milk unless you ask; *infusiones* (herbal teas) can be found in most places.

Essentials A-Z

Accident and emergency
General emergencies 112.
Ambulance 061. **Fire** 080.
Police 091.

Electricity
220V. A round 2-pin plug is used (European standard).

Embassies and consulates
For a list of Spanish embassies and consulates, see www.maec.es.

Health
Medical facilities in Andalucía are very good. However, EU citizens should make sure they have the **European Health Insurance Card** (EHIC) to prove reciprocal rights to medical care. These are available free of charge in the UK from the Department of Health (www.dh.gov.uk) or post offices.

Non-EU citizens should consider travel insurance to cover emergency and routine medical needs; be sure that it covers any sports or activities you may do. Check for reciprocal cover with your private or public health scheme first.

Water is safe to drink, but isn't always pleasant, so many travellers (and locals) stick to bottled water. The **sun** in southern Spain can be harsh, so take precautions to avoid heat exhaustion and sunburn.

Many medications that require a prescription in other countries are available over the counter at pharmacies in Spain. Pharmacists are highly trained and usually speak some English. In medium-sized towns and cities, at least one pharmacy is open 24 hrs; this is performed on a rota system (posted in the window of all pharmacies and listed in local newspapers).

No vaccinations are needed.

Money
Currency and exchange
Exchange rates £1=€1.21, US$1=€0.73 (Jan 2014). For up-to-the-minute exchange rates visit www.xe.com.

Since 2002, Spain has been part of the eurozone. The euro (€) is divided into 100 *céntimos*. Euro notes are standard across the whole zone and come in denominations of 5, 10, 20, 50, 100, and the rarely seen 200 and 500. Coins have one standard face and one national face; all coins are, however, acceptable in all countries. The coins are slightly difficult to tell apart when you're not used to them. The coppers are 1, 2 and 5 cent pieces, the golds are 10, 20 and 50, and the silver/gold combinations are €1 and €2.

ATMs and banks
The best way to get money in Spain is by plastic. ATMs are plentiful and accept all the major international debit and credit cards. The Spanish bank won't charge for the transaction, though they will charge a mark-up on the exchange rate, but beware of

your own bank hitting you for a hefty fee: check with them before leaving home. Even if they do, it's likely to be a better deal than changing cash over a counter. Pre-paid currency cards are another practical option.

Banks are usually open Mon-Fri (and Sat in winter) 0830-1430 and many change foreign money (sometimes only the central branch in a town will do it). Commission rates vary widely; it's usually best to change large amounts, as there's often a minimum commission. The website www. moneysavingexpert.com has a good rundown on the most economical ways of accessing cash while travelling.

Cost of living

Spain is much more expensive than it was, and for the traveller is no longer a money-saving destination. Nevertheless, it still offers value for money, and you can get by cheaply if you forgo a few luxuries. If you're travelling as a pair, staying in cheap *pensiones*, eating a set meal at lunchtime, travelling short distances and snacking on tapas in the evenings, €65 per person per day is reasonable. If you camp and grab picnic lunches from shops, you could reduce this somewhat. In a good *hostal* or cheap hotel and using a car, €150 a day and you'll not be counting pennies; €300 per day and you'll be very comfy indeed unless you're staying in 5-star accommodation.

Accommodation in Málaga province is significantly more expensive in summer than winter, particularly on the coast, where hotels and *hostales*

in seaside towns are overpriced. The news isn't great for the solo traveller; single rooms tend not to be particularly good value and they are in short supply. Prices range from 60% to 80% of the double/twin price; some establishments even charge the full rate. If you're going to be staying in 3- to 5-star hotels, booking them ahead on internet discount sites can save you money.

Public transport is generally cheap; intercity bus services are quick and low-priced, though the new fast trains are expensive. If you're hiring a car, Málaga is the cheapest place in Andalucía. Petrol costs have skyrocketed: standard unleaded petrol is around 155 cents per litre. In some places, particularly in tourist areas, you may be charged up to 20% more to sit outside a restaurant. It's also worth checking if the 10% IVA (sales tax) is included in menu prices, especially in the more expensive restaurants; it should say on the menu.

Opening hours
Business hours Mon-Fri 1000-1400, 1700-2000; Sat 1000-1400. **Banks** Mon-Fri, plus Sat in winter, 0830-1430. **Government offices** Mornings only.

Safety
Andalucía is a very safe place to travel. There's been a crackdown on tourist crime in recent years and even large places like Málaga feel much safer than their equivalents in, say, England.

What tourist crime there is tends to be of the opportunistic kind. Robberies from parked cars (particularly those with foreign plates) or snatch-and-run thefts from vehicles stopped at traffic lights are not unknown, and the occasional mugger operates in Málaga. Keep car doors locked when driving in cities. If parking in a city or a popular hiking zone, make it clear there's nothing worth robbing in a car by opening the glove compartment.

If you are unfortunate enough to be robbed, you should report the theft immediately at the nearest police station, as insurance companies will require a copy of the *denuncia* (police statement).

Tax

Nearly all goods and services in Spain are subject to a value-added tax (IVA). This is 10% for things like hotels and restaurant meals, but is 21% on other things. IVA is normally included in the stated prices. You're technically entitled to claim it back if you're a non-EU citizen, for purchases over €90. If you're buying something pricey, make sure you get an official stamped receipt (*factura*) clearly showing the IVA component, as well as your name and passport number; you can claim the amount back at major airports on departure. Some shops will have a form to smooth the process.

Time

1 hr ahead of GMT.

Tipping

Tipping in Spain is far from compulsory. A 10% tip would be considered extremely generous in a restaurant; 3% to 5% is more usual. It's rare for a service charge to be added to a bill. Waiters don't expect tips but in bars and cafés people will often leave small change, especially for table service. Taxi drivers don't expect a tip, but will be pleased to receive one.

Visas and immigration

EU citizens and those from countries within the Schengen agreement can enter Spain freely. UK and Irish citizens will need to carry a passport, while an identity card suffices for other EU/Schengen nationals. Citizens of Australia, the USA, Canada, New Zealand, several Latin American countries and Israel can enter without a visa for up to 90 days. Other citizens will require a visa, obtainable from Spanish consulates or embassies. These are usually issued quickly and are valid for all Schengen countries. The basic visa is valid for 90 days, and you'll need 2 passport photos, proof of funds covering your stay, and possibly evidence of medical cover (ie insurance).

For extensions of visas, apply to an *oficina de extranjeros* in a major city (usually in the *comisaría*, main police station).

Weights and measures

Metric.

Contents

Málaga & Costa del Sol

Málaga

Though no more than an airport for millions of sunseekers, Málaga is an important Spanish port and city with plenty to offer, perhaps more than the rest of its province's coast put together. Once bypassed by tourists en route to the beach resorts, these days Andalucía's second largest city is a destination in its own right, with the Picasso Museum as the main crowd-puller. Málaga's charm is focused in the historic city centre, with its majestic cathedral surrounded by sun-baked ochre buildings and narrow pedestrian streets. The long town beach is pretty clean, and there's plenty of good-value accommodation. The city is looking very spruce these days, with the designer boutiques of its central streets overlooked by the Moorish castle. It's also got a great tapas scene and one of Andalucía's liveliest fiestas.

Background

Málaga has a long history dating back to the Phoenicians, who founded a settlement called *Malaka*, a word derived from *malac*, meaning to salt fish. Málaga became a busy trading port during Roman times, exporting minerals and agricultural produce from the interior. From the eighth century, Málaga was occupied by the Moors, when it was the main port for the province of Granada. It was they, under Yusef I, who built the Gibralfaro fortress in the 14th century. The city fell to the Catholics in 1487 after a long and violent siege.

After the expulsion of the morisco population in the mid-16th century, the fortunes of Málaga declined. It was not until the 19th century, when an agricultural-based revival began, that the situation improved. Gradually, the Costa capital began to become a favoured wintering place for wealthy *madrileños*. During the Civil War, Málaga supported the Republicans and the city suffered from the vicious fighting, which included an Italian bombardment that destroyed part of its ancient centre.

Over the last 50 years, mass tourism has transformed the neighbouring Costa del Sol, but has thankfully had little effect on the city itself, which remains intrinsically Spanish.

Places in Málaga → *For listings, see pages 25-31.*

Most of the places of interest in Málaga are contained within an atmospheric area of 19th-century streets and squares north of the main east-west thoroughfare. Look out for the new Museo de Málaga, whose archaeological and art collections are to be located in the sturdy Palacio de la Aduana near the Roman theatre; it's due to open in 2015.

The cathedral and around

ⓘ *C Molina Lario s/n, T952-215917. Mon-Fri 1000-1800, Sat 1000-1700, Sun 1400-1800. €5, free Sun.*

Málaga's cathedral, as with many others in Andalucía, was built on the site of a mosque and dates from the 16th century, with numerous modifications at later dates. One of its two towers was never completed, giving it a lopsided appearance, leading to the nickname of *La Manquita*, or the one-armed lady. The interior is both Gothic and Renaissance, while the exterior is typical 18th-century Baroque, aside from a particularly fine Gothic doorway in Plateresque style that dates from the early 16th century.

The highlight of the interior is, without doubt, the **choir**. Behind the stalls are some superb carvings of saints, 42 of which are attributed to Pedro de Mena around 1662. (De Mena's house, now a museum devoted to the painter Revello de Toro, is located in a back street about 500 m from the cathedral.) Rearing above the choir stalls are two 18th-century organs. The north entrance, the **Portal of the Chains**, which is usually closed except for Semana Santa processions, is surrounded by a fine screen, carved in mahogany and cedar by Francisco Flores in 1772, with the coats of arms of Felipe II. The admission fee to the cathedral also includes entry to the run-down *museo* near the entrance door, which contains the usual vestments and silver.

There are a number of interesting churches in Málaga centre, the most outstanding being the **Iglesia del Sagrario**, adjacent to the cathedral, with a superb Plateresque *retablo*, and **Nuestra Señora de la Victoria** ⓘ *Tue-Sat 1000-1300, €2*, in Calle Victoria, which has further work by de Mena.

Next to the cathedral on Plaza del Obispo, surrounded by open-air bars and cafés, is the 18th-century **Palacio del Obispo**, or Episcopal Palace, with one of the most beautiful façades in the city.

Museo Picasso Málaga

ⓘ *C San Agustín 8, T952-127600, www.museopicassomalaga.org. Tue-Thu 1000-2000, Fri-Sat 1000-2100, Sun 1000-2000. Also open Mon 1000-2000 in Jul and Aug. Collection €6, exhibitions €4.50, both €9.*

This museum has made a significant impact on Málaga; it's put it on the map as a destination in its own right rather than merely a transport hub for the

Costa del Sol. The museum is set in the beautiful Buenavista palace, and the juxtaposition of Renaissance architecture and modern painting has been artfully realized. On display are some 150 Picasso works, mostly donated by

Málaga

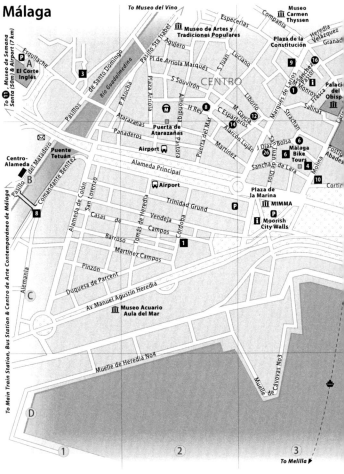

Where to stay 🛏	Don Curro **6** *B3*	Suite Novotel Málaga
AC Hotel Málaga	Eurostars Astoria **8** *B1*	Centro **3** *A1*
Palacio **10** *B3*	Molina Lario **4** *B3*	
Alameda **1** *C2*	Oasis Málaga **2** *A4*	**Restaurants** 🍴
California **11** *D6*	Parador de Gibralfaro **12** *B6*	Antigua Casa Guardia **2** *B2*
Casa Babylon **5** *A6*	Room Mate Larios **9** *A3*	Bar Lo Güeno **12** *A3*

his daughter-in-law and grandson. Most phases of the artist's trajectory are represented, from formal portraiture – *Olga con Mantilla* (1917) is a portrait of his first wife – to Blue Period and Cubist works, and many from the later stages

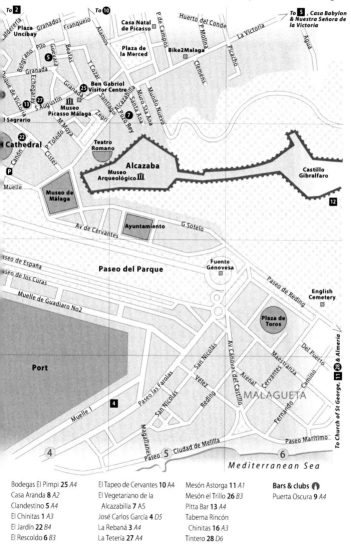

of Picasso's life. It's an excellent opportunity to see a lot of his *oeuvre* in one place. There are regular temporary exhibitions running on the Picasso theme or focusing on contemporaries; there is also a café and bookshop here.

Not far away, you can visit the **Casa Natal de Picasso** ① *T952-060215, www.fundacionpicasso.es, daily 0930-2000, closed Tue from Nov-Mar, €2,* Picasso's birthplace and now the headquarters of the Picasso Foundation. It is located in the large Plaza de la Merced and has several Picasso ceramics and lithographs. There's also various personal objects that belonged to the artist's parents and regular temporary exhibitions in the adjacent building.

The Alcazaba
① *T952-216005, Apr-Oct Mon 0900-2000, Tue-Sun 0900-2015, Nov-Mar Mon 0900-1800, Tue-Sun 0830-1930. €2.20 (€3.55 joint entry price with Castillo Gibralfaro).*
This former fortress and palace was begun by the Moors in the 700s, but most of the structure dates from the mid-11th century. The site was originally occupied by both the Phoenicians and the Romans, and there remains a considerable amount of Roman masonry in the walls. The Alcazaba suffered badly during the Catholic Reconquest, but was restored in the 1930s. Today, it consists of a series of terraced, fortified walls and fine gateways, laid out with gardens and running water in typical Moorish style. From the terraces of the main palace building there are fine views over the port and the city.

The **Castillo Gibralfaro** ① *Nov-Mar daily 0900-1800, Apr-Oct 0900-2100, €2.20 (€3.55 joint-entry price with Alcazaba),* literally 'Lighthouse Hill', is a ruined Moorish castle built by Yusef I of Granada in the early 14th century. It is linked to the Alcazaba below by parallel walls. A path leads up to it from the right side of the Alcazaba; you can also approach it by the road that leads from the city up towards the *parador* via Calle Victoria. Alternatively, take the No 35 bus from Paseo del Parque.

Located close to the entrance of the Alcazaba, the **Teatro Romano** ① *May-Sep Tue 1200-2000, Wed-Sat 0900-2030, Sun 1000-1600, Oct-Apr Tue 1000-1800, Wed-Sat 0900-1900, Sun 1000-1600, free,* was built in the early first century AD and used for a couple of centuries. Much of the stone was later used by the Moors for their fortresses above, but restoration has left the theatre looking rather spruce. There's a small interpretation centre and information in Spanish and English.

The waterfront
From the Alcazaba, the tree-lined **Paseo del Parque** is a delightful avenue that leads down to the port area and a place of blessed relief on hot summer days. At the western end of the port area is the **Museo Acuario Aula del Mar** ① *Av Manuel Augustín de la Heredia, T952-229287, www.auladelmar.info, Oct-Jun Mon-Fri 1000-1400, 1630-2130, Sat-Sun 1000-1400, 1630-2330, Jul-Sep 1100-*

1400, 1700-midnight daily, €7, children €5, a marine museum with aquaria and some underwater caves containing turtles, octopuses and coral. The museum runs marine ecology courses and boat excursions in Málaga Bay. Near here, on the harbour's eastern shore, Muelle 1 is a chic new shopping and leisure precinct that's great for strolling.

East of here stretches the city's clean sandy beach, where numerous *chiringuitos* vie for the custom of lovers of seafood and cold beer in the summer months.

A couple of blocks back from the beach, the **English Cemetery** ⓘ *Tue-Sat 1030-1400, 1030-1300, closed Tue-Wed in Jul and Aug, free*, is a beautiful spot that owes its existence to the days when infidels (ie non-Catholics) were buried on the beach, making gruesome reappearances courtesy of storms or hungry dogs. In the mid-18th century, a British consul persuaded the authorities to allow him to start an English cemetery. Look for the small **Church of St George**, a block past the bullring on Paseo de Reding.

From here, a path leads into the leafy walled cemetery, which is a haven of peace. The inscriptions on the gravestones make absorbing reading; there are graves here of many nationalities, the earlier ones covered in shells. The writer Gerald Brenan is buried here alongside his wife, the poet Gamel Woolsey; he had wanted his body to be donated to medical science, but was so well respected by the *malagueños* that none of the members of the anatomy faculty could bring themselves to touch him; he finally arrived here in 2000, some 14 years after his death.

Other museums and galleries

Another of Málaga's Moorish curiosities, **Puerta de Atarazañas**, is at the entrance to the city market. This was originally the gateway into the Moorish dockyard and it displays the crest of the Nasrid dynasty. The market is vibrant and colourful and well worth investigating.

Anyone interested in social history should see the **Museo de Artes y Costumbres Populares** ⓘ *C Pasillo Santa Isabel 10, www.museoartespopulares. com, Mon-Fri 1000-1700, Sat 1000-1400, €4*, which is located by the dried-up bed of the Río Guadalmedina, a two-minute walk from the Alameda. Look for the inn sign labelled Mesón de Victoria, as this museum is housed in an old 17th-century hostelry with typical flower-filled patio. The museum consists of a haphazard collection of everyday items from several centuries ago, including fishing boats, an olive press, guns, farming implements and a range of household relics.

The **Centro de Arte Contemporáneo de Málaga** ⓘ *C Alemania s/n, www. cacmalaga.org, Tue-Sun 1000-2000, summer 1000-1400 and 1700-2100, free*, is dedicated to contemporary art in all its forms. Outside the entrance, a sculpture of a figure with crumpled shirt and trousers (*Man Moving* by German artist Stephen Balkenholl) sets the tone of *vanguardismo*, which includes contemplative photographic studies and paintings, some of them immense in size and all given optimum display space in white, bright exhibition halls. The aim of the centre is to pioneer new artistic trends through four exhibitions which run concurrently: two temporary shows, another for up-and-coming local artists and a changing, permanent exhibition of pieces selected by renowned modern artists.

Another worthwhile gallery is the excellent **Museo Carmen Thyssen** ⓘ *C Compañía 10, www.carmenthyssenmalaga.org, Tue-Sun 1000-2000, €6*, in the centre of town. The focus here is on the 19th century in Spain. It was a turbulent century, but you won't see that here: much of the work features romanticized depictions of an idealized Andalucía. Gypsies, flamenco, Easter processions, lovers at window grilles, inns, mules, priests and bullfights: all the stereotypes beautifully represented.

The **Museo Interactivo de la Música de Málaga** (**MIMMA**) ⓘ *Plaza de la Marina s/n, www.musicaenaccion.com, Mon 1000-1400, Tue-Sun 1000-1400, 1600-2000, €4*, is an atmospheric underground space below Plaza de la Marina, the hub of Málaga. Its collection of musical instruments, variety of recordings and changing exhibitions among the foundations of the Nasrid city walls focus on both traditional and contemporary musical trends.

Málaga's **Museo del Vino** ⓘ *Plaza de los Viñeros 1, www.museovinomalaga. com, €5, Mon-Fri 1000-1700, Sat 1000-1400*, is located in a restored *palacio* a short walk northwest of the old centre. The modern but slightly functional display takes you through the history and actuality of winemaking in the Málaga area through a series of display panels in Spanish. Guided tours leave every 30 minutes for no extra cost and guides speak English. The price of admission includes a tasting of a dry and a sweet wine.

Concepción Botanical Gardens
ⓘ *4 km north of the city centre, T952-252148, laconcepcion.malaga.eu. Tue-Sun 0930-2030, until 1730 Oct-Mar, last entry 1 hr before. €5.20, guided tour, with multilingual guides, for 1½ hrs. Easy access, well signposted off the Málaga–Antequera autovía, just off the Ronda de Málaga; bus No 61 Sat-Sun, otherwise get bus No 2 and walk 10 mins north.*

These botanical gardens are well worth a visit, particularly as a change from the heat of the city or the beach. The gardens have an interesting history, being created over 150 years ago by Amalia Heredia and her husband, the American George Loring, a mining tycoon, who later became the Marquis of Casa-Loring. They collected plants from many parts of the world and also accumulated an important archaeological collection. The visit leads to a mirador giving stunning views over Málaga (the cathedral and castle are clearly visible) and the enormous stone dam of La Concepción reservoir.

Málaga listings

For hotel and restaurant price codes and other relevant information, see pages 6-12.

◉ Where to stay

Málaga *p18, map p20*
There's a good range of accommodation for all budgets in the central area around the Alameda near the port. Prices go up in summer; some cheaper options at this time include university residences, which you can reserve via www.booking.com.

€€€€ Parador de Gibralfaro, Paseo García del Olmo, T952-221902, www.parador.es. In a dreamy setting, surrounded by pine trees, next to the Moorish castle with panoramic views. The rooms are simply yet tastefully decorated with warm colours, woven rugs and terracotta tiles. There are private entrances and sun terraces. The restaurant dishes up regional and international fare. Booking essential.

€€€ AC Hotel Málaga Palacio, C Cortina del Muelle 1, T952-215185, www.marriott.com. This grand central hotel offers excellent facilities in a great location. Rooms are slick and modern with beige and wood furnishings and steely grey marble bathrooms. Extra appeal is added by the free minibar, pool and great restaurant terrace with views across town.

€€€ Don Curro, C Sancha de Lara 7, T952-227200, www.hoteldoncurro. com. Superb situation on a pedestrian side street off C Marqués de Larios, near the cathedral with a grand marble-clad entrance. Rooms are faultless and staff make the effort to make your stay a pleasant one. There's a wood-panelled lounge with fireplace and the surprising addition of a bingo parlour. Prices drop considerably at weekends. Parking.

€€€ Hotel Molina Lario, C Molina Lario 20, T952-062002, www.hotel molinalario.com. Near the cathedral, this 4-star choice successfully spreads itself to appeal to both the work traveller, with sleek design and business facilities, and families, with kid-friendly staff, and a rooftop pool and terrace to relax. The rooms are spacious, sparklingly clean and stylishly modern; those facing the street are the most appealing. Service is excellent. Recommended.

€€€ Room Mate Larios, Marqués de Larios 2, T952-222200, www.room-matehotels.com. This has an upbeat feel to match its top location on Málaga's swanky pedestrian shopping street. The cheerful yet elegant decor features black and white tiles, cream, maroon and warm-toned furnishings and plenty of light wood. Try for a room overlooking the bustling Plaza de la Constitución, although it can be noisy on a Sat night. Free internet and Wi-Fi. You can get some very good deals on the website, depending on the date.

€€€ Suite Novotel Málaga Centro, C San Jacinto 7, T952-614296, www. accorhotels.com. Set behind Corte Inglés just across the riverbed from the centre, this new hotel offers peace and quiet in its attractive and comfortable modern rooms, which come with a microwave and tea-making facilities. The sofa folds out into a bed, making it a good family option. It's a pleasant stroll into town, and you can park pretty easily around here.

€€ Eurostars Astoria, C Comandante Benítez 5, T951-014300, www.eurostarshotels.com. Slick 3-star hotel near the Contemporary Art Gallery. Rooms are spacious with plenty of gleaming marble and light wood. Excellent value for the price with many extras including hydromassage in the en suite bathrooms and internet access in all rooms. You can get cheaper deals on hotel-booking websites. It's near Alameda train station, for trains to the airport.

€€ Hotel Alameda, C Casas de Campos 3, T952-222099, www.hotelalamedamalaga.com. A plush red carpet leads you to your smell-the-cleanliness room at this 8th-floor hotel in a handy location between the port and the Alameda. It's run by an obliging couple with English spoken; there's free Wi-Fi and parking available.

€€ Hotel California, Paseo de Sancha 17, T952-215164, www.hotelcalifornia.net. Near the beach at the eastern end of town, this is a friendly hotel with unremarkable but spacious rooms despite the ominous name. The staff are very helpful and it represents significant value for this coastline.

€ Casa Babylon, C Pedro de Quejana 3, T952-267228, www.casababylonhostel.com. Laid-back but facility packed, this backpackers in a suburban house offers comfortable new bunks, an instant Málaga social life, cheap beer and free internet. The only downside is it's a bit of a trek from the centre of the action. Breakfast included.

€ Oasis Málaga, C San Telmo 14, T952-005116, www.oasismalaga.com. Chock-full of traveller-friendly features, this upbeat, good-looking hostel has a bar, free internet, a kitchen, and an instant social life on the roof terrace.

❼ Restaurants

Málaga p18, map p20
There are some superb restaurants where you can enjoy traditional local specialities, such as *fritura malagueña* (fried fish), washed down with Málaga's famous wine, a sherry-like substance that comes in sweet and dry varieties. Many of the best fish restaurants as well as *chiringuitos* on the sea can be found in the suburbs of Pedregalejo and El Palo.

€€€ José Carlos García, Muelle 1, T952 003 588, www.restaurantejcg.com. Málaga's standout gourmet dining experience is in a crisply attractive location at the new harbour development. The degustation menu blends traditional Adalucían ingredients with new Spanish molecular gastronomy techniques to great effect. Service is helpful, but you'll need to book ahead. Recommended.

€€€ Restaurante El Chinitas, C Moreno Monroy 4, T952-210972, www.elchinitas.com. A traditional restaurant in a century-old building with paintings of local bullfighters lining the walls. Dishes are predictably macho with oxtail a speciality, plus calf sirloin, sweet Picasso sole and *serrano* ham.

€€ Bar Lo Güeno, C Marín García 9, T952-223048, www.logueno.es. This cosy backstreet bar and its restaurant opposite make a great place to start an exploration of Málaga's eating scene. Sit outside on the street or elbow your way up to the L-shaped counter to admire the stunning array of tapas, mostly displayed for your viewing pleasure. They range from warming stew-type choices in pans above the counter to refreshingly crisp seafood salads. Service is friendly, and prices generous for the quality.

€€ Bodegas El Pimpi, C Granada 62, T952-228990, www.bodegabarel pimpi.com. Near the Picasso Museum, this labyrinthine former wine warehouse offers atmosphere in spades, with local sweet and dry drops in barrels signed by famous folk who've been here. If you can grab a table (it's big but often packed), you can snack on traditional Andalucían dishes, but the ambience is probably better than the food. There's a pleasant terrace around the back opposite the Roman theatre.

€€ Clandestino, C Niño de Guevara 3, T952-219390, www.clandestino malaga.com. Daily 1300-0100. This inventive and intensely popular brasserie can resemble a student canteen at first sight, with its chunky wooden tables, relaxed bohemian ambience and scurrying staff. Don't be fooled, as the cuisine is classy and inventive; they aim high, and if they don't always reach, they still comfortably clear most of the places around here.

€€ El Rescoldo, C Bolsa 7, T952-226919, www.grupotrillo.es. Offering appealing shaded tables on a pedestrian street junction, this is a relaxing place to eat. Tasty meats are best preceded by shared plates of grilled vegetables, cheese or Iberian ham. Pass on the outrageously pricey Norwegian bottled water though and go for the local stuff. Online booking makes reservations easy.

€€ El Tapeo de Cervantes, C Cárcer 8, T952 609 458, www.eltapeode cervantes.com. Intimate and charming, one of Málaga's best tapas options is a couple of blocks north of Plaza de la Merced. You might have to wait for one of the few tables, but it's worth it, with excellent traditional dishes backed up by some highly original creations.

€€ La Rebaná, C Molina Lario 4, T952-608534, www.larebana.com. Near the cathedral, this handsome split-level restaurant and tapas place is a winner. Stylishly presented original cuisine delivers plenty of quality (if not quantity), with delicacies like smoked palometa (a fish), a selection of foies, and tasty daily specials delighting a smartly dressed Málaga crowd. Smaller tapas portions are *molletes* or *rebanadas*, a piece of toasted bread with a variety of elaborate toppings.

€€ Mesón Astorga, C Gerona 11, T952 346 832, www.mesonastorga. com. It's worth the walk out to this welcoming place near the train station for an excellent Málaga dining experience. Top-quality produce, including great grilled meats and fresh fish, is backed up by interesting wines and a genuinely Spanish atmosphere. Recommended.

€€ Mesón el Trillo, C Don Juan Diaz 4, T952-603920. This warm and convivial spot is another great tapas offering. Excellent wines are available by the glass, and there's a big range of bar food, from *trillos* served on toasted bread, to *revueltos* and delicious chopped steaks. There's also a restaurant menu, served in the spacious interior or on the terrace, but not quite as much love goes into the food, it seems.

€€ Taberna Rincón Chinitas, Pasaje Chinitas 9, T952-223029. For the best *berenjenas con miel* (deep-fried aubergines with honey) and excellent seafood head to this tiny *taberna* on one of the most atmospheric streets in the city and once a haunt of Lorca and friends. There are romantic tables on the street.

€€ Tintero, Playa del Dedo, El Palo, T952-204464, www.restaurante eltintero.com. One of the most entertaining restaurants (with another branch near Cártama). Waiters bear dishes non-stop into the dining area, shouting what they've got on offer. If you fancy it, grab it from them; nearly all dishes have a standard price. Fried fish is the main thing to try here. It's fast, entertaining and extremely noisy.

€ Antigua Casa Guardia, Alameda 18, T952-214680, on the corner of C Pastora. Founded in 1840, this wonderfully atmospheric bar seems to have changed little since then. It opens at 0900 in the morning and starts filling old men's glasses with delicious Málaga wines from the row of barrels behind the bar. A little seafood stall dishes out prawns and mussels as the perfect accompaniment to a chilled *seco*. A photograph on the wall shows a youthful Picasso knocking one back here. Recommended.

€ El Vegetariano de la Alcazabilla, C Pozo del Rey 5, T952-214858. One of several vegetarian restaurants around town, this has a handy location at the foot of the Alcazaba and a pleasant quiet terrace. Home-made wholemeal pasta, plenty of salads, vegan dishes and a very tasty mushroom *pil-pil*. On weekdays there's a generous mixed plate for not much cash.

€ Pitta Bar, C Echegaray 8, T952-608675. Tucked around the corner from the Picasso Museum, you'll find Middle Eastern tapas like falafel, hummus, *baba ghanoush* and tabbouleh. Great for vegetarians. There's a terrace on the street too.

Cafés

Casa Aranda, C Herrería del Rey 1. At certain moments Málaga seems to go eerily quiet; that usually means it's time for chocolate and *churros* at this venerable central café. Sure enough, you'll find it packed to the seams with people dipping away. Morning and early evening are accepted times for this; there are also other decent breakfast choices.

El Jardín, C Cister 2, www.eljardin malaga.com. Tucked behind the cathedral, this large and handsome café has a little terrace and great art nouveau ambience. It's a place to go for a coffee, rather than tapas (which are unremarkable), or to take in the live music at weekends.

La Tetería, C San Agustín 9, near the Museo Picasso, www.la-teteria.com. This is a popular teahouse that, as well as numerous infusions, has outdoor tables and a range of sandwiches, salads and pastries.

🎧 Bars and clubs

Málaga *p18, map p20*
The main central nightlife zone is just north of C Granada in the streets around C Luis de Velázquez. Plaza Merced also has some options, while on Plaza Marqués del Vado del Maestre, just off C Calderería in the centre, there are also several bars, whose customers merge outside on the square. There is a host of disco-bars south of the bullring, in the Malagueta area, whereas nightlife in the summer months tends to spill out towards El Palo and its beachside discos.

Puerta Oscura, C Molina Lario 5, T952-221900, www.puertaoscura malaga.com. One of the classiest in Málaga, this 19th-century bar-café has chandeliers, alcoves and classical music. It's the best place for that late-night coffee and liquor. Recommended.

✵ Festivals

Málaga *p18, map p20*
Easter Semana Santa, when religious brotherhoods organize daily processions with huge and elaborate floats carrying sacred *paso* figures through the streets of the city. It's one of Spain's best Easter celebrations.
23 Jun San Juan, sees huge bonfires on the beach, live concerts and all-night partying.
16 Jul Virgen del Carmen's effigy is taken by a procession of boats out to sea by fishermen.
Aug Feria, with bullfights, flamenco, processions and fireworks. There are 2 venues: during the day festivities take place in the streets surrounding C Marqués de Larios; in the evening it moves to the fairgrounds on the outskirts of the city where one of Spain's biggest parties kicks off night after night. All the *casetas* are open to the public, and most serve food as well as drinks.

🛍 Shopping

Málaga *p18, map p20*
The main shopping area is west of the cathedral and north of the Alameda Principal and in the streets around the Plaza de la Constitución. The **Larios shopping centre**, located between **El Corte Inglés** and the bus station, has over 100 shops, a hypermarket and a multi-cinema.

⚙ What to do

Málaga *p18, map p20*
Baths
El Hammam, C Tomás de Cózar 13, T952-212327, http://malaga. hammamalandalus.com. Daily 1000-2400. These traditional Arab baths are housed in an attractive 18th-century building in Málaga's old Jewish quarter. They are segregated by sex, and it's advisable to book your slot ahead. There are various massage treatments too. From €30.

Bike tours and hire
Bike2Malaga, C Victoria 15, T650-677063, www.bike2malaga.com. Near the Plaza Merced, these people offer bike hire with a variety of different 2-wheelers and also give guided city tours.
Málaga Bike Tours, Pasaje La Trini 6, T606-978513, www.malagabike tours.eu. These people take you on good-natured 2-wheeled tours of town. They also rent bikes for €5/10 for a half/full day.

Football
Málaga have a lot of support, partly from the expat crowd. Games are held at the **Estadio de Fútbol La Rosaleda**, Av de Martiricos, T952-614374, www.malagacf.es.

Golf
There are over 40 golf courses along the Costa del Sol to the west of the city. The nearest, and the oldest course on the coast, is **Real Club de Camp de Málaga**, T952-376677, www.rccm-golf.com, 4 km east of Torremolinos. It's state owned and attached to the Parador de Golf hotel.

⊖ Transport

Málaga *p18, map p20*
Air
Málaga has a busy airport from which **Iberia** and its subsidiaries, as well as **Vueling** and **Ryanair** run internal flights to several Spanish cities. Numerous budget airlines from all over Europe fly to Málaga, some only in the summer. See Getting to Málaga and the Costa del Sol, page 6, for more details.

Bus
A complete timetable is available from the tourist office. The main bus station is on Paseo Tilos, T952-350061. There are hourly buses to **Granada** (2 hrs). Buses to **Sevilla** leave a few times daily (2 hrs 45 mins). Buses to **Córdoba** leave 4 times daily (3 hrs), and there are many buses along the coast in both directions.

Car hire
All the main international firms have offices at the airport. Local Spanish firms are also represented. As ever, the best deals are to be found online via broker websites. Smaller firms have their offices on the airport approach road, to which they will transport customers by minibus (allow 30 mins for this when departing). Other offices cluster around the train station.

Ferries

There are daily sailings to **Melilla**, the Spanish enclave in North Africa. The crossing takes around 8 hrs. For further information contact **Trasmediterránea**, C Juan Díaz 4, T902-454645, www.trasmediterranea.es.

Taxi

There are taxi ranks at the bus and train stations and on Alameda Principal. **Radio Taxi**, T952-327950. One of several companies.

Trains

The RENFE station is in the southwest of town. There are 11 daily **AVE** trains to **Madrid** (2 hrs 40 mins, €96), which travel via **Córdoba**, also served by cheaper trains (1 hr, €27-42). There's a daily train to **Ronda** (1¾ hrs, €14), leaving at 1843 and stopping at **Alora** and **El Chorro**. There are 6 daily slow trains and 6 daily fast trains to **Sevilla** (2 hrs 30 min, €123; 1 hr 55 mins, €42) as well as services to other Andalucían cities.

The **Fuengirola**–Málaga *cercanía* line is planned eventually to extend to **Marbella** and Estepona in the west, and Nerja in the east and has another branch running north to **Alora**. Purchase tickets from the machines on the platform.

❻ Directory

Málaga *p18, map p20*
Banks Banks are mostly concentrated at the west end of the Alameda Principal. There are a few change shops in the central area, but the commission can be high. **Medical services Pharmacy: Farmacia Caffarena**, Alameda Principal 2, cnr C Larios, T952-212858. Open 24 hrs. **Post** Av de Andalucía, T952-359008, almost opposite El Corte Inglés.

East from Málaga

Traditionally more Spanish in character, the eastern Costa del Sol is facing a rapidly increasing influx of tourists and retirees from northern Europe and is changing its nature quickly. Nevertheless, Nerja is attractive, with less ribbon development than the west of the province and plenty of character.

Nerja → *For listings, see pages 34-36.*

Despite rapid recent growth, Nerja, some 50 km east of its provincial capital, still retains considerable charm in its narrow, winding streets and spectacular location on a low cliff, backed by impressive mountains. There are sandy coves, long beaches and, despite a spiralling increase in residential tourism, most of the new buildings and *urbanizaciones* have been aesthetically designed. Nerja's caves east of town pull the crowds and make a dazzling venue for the annual summer festival. Nerja also has excellent places to stay and eat.

Getting around Nerja is small enough for most places to be reached on foot, and it's relatively easy to park on the edges of town or at the underground car park in the centre (follow signs for Balcón de Europa). It's pricey but very handy. Near here, just across from Balcón de Europa, the **tourist office** ⓘ *C Carmen 1, T952-521531, www.nerja.org, Mon-Sat 1000-1400, 1630-2030 (winter 1500-1845), Sun 1000-1400,* occupies the ground floor of the town hall.

Background
Nerja started life as the Moorish settlement of *Narixa*, but an earthquake in 1884 destroyed much of the town and no Moorish constructions survived. For centuries the inhabitants eked out a living by making silk, growing sugar cane and fishing. None of these activities thrive today and the sugar refining buildings are part of the industrial archaeology. Nerja is famous in Spain for having been the setting for the iconic early 1980s TV series *Verano Azul*.

Places in Nerja
Today, the local economy is largely reliant on tourism. There is also a large foreign community who have made Nerja their permanent home. Architectural controls here mean that there are few high-rise hotels and the centre is still old fashioned with narrow winding streets flanked by bars, souvenir and speciality shops.

At the heart of the town is the famous **Balcón de Europa**, a balmy, palmy promenade with magnificent views over the rocky coastline. Beware, however, of the inflated prices charged in the bars and restaurants around the Balcón. To the west of here is the whitewashed **Church of El Salvador**, dwarfed by its Norfolk pine. It has elements of *mudéjar* and baroque work, plus an interesting mural representing the Annunciation on a Nerja beach. There are still a few fishing boats on the **Playa Calahonda**, just east of the Balcón, but the most popular beach, just out of sight behind the headland, is **Burriana**, which is packed during the summer and offers a whole range of watersports, ranging from waterskiing to kitesurfing.

Around Nerja

Cuevas de Nerja

ⓘ *Ctra de Maro s/n, T952-529520, www.cuevadenerja.es, daily 1000-1400 and 1600-1830 (1000-1930 in Jul/Aug). €8.50, 6-12s €4.50. The caves are just above the N340, and clearly signposted from it. Parking costs €1. There are regular buses from Nerja, or it's a 30-min walk.*

These limestone caves were discovered in 1959 by a group of local schoolboys on a bat-hunting expedition and are now a major tourist destination, with busloads rolling up every day of the year. The most important finds were the wall paintings, probably Upper Palaeolithic in age and largely of animals, believed to be part of a magical rite to ensure success in hunting and guarantee the fertility of domestic animals. Regrettably, the paintings are not on public view. The guided visit takes just under an hour; the lighting of the caves and the piped music may appear to some visitors to be somewhat overdone, but the limestone features are genuinely awe-inspiring. The caves are far more extensive than you get to appreciate on the tour, but you can get to grips with further sections by booking a day's caving (October to June, booking via the above number or website). The day costs €500 for up to 10 people – ask for dates when you can join a group (over 14s only) and includes drinks, sandwiches, equipment, guide and around seven hours of exploration. In the summer season, the main chamber of the caves is used as an auditorium for a festival of music. There is a restaurant with a terrace giving superb views along the coast.

East from Málaga listings

For hotel and restaurant price codes and other relevant information, see pages 6-12.

● Where to stay

Nerja *p32*

There is a good choice of accommodation to suit all pockets. It is best to book in advance during summer and Semana Santa.

€€€€ Parador de Nerja, C Almuñécar 8, T952-520050, www.parador.es. The only disappointment here is that, unlike many *paradores*, the building is not a historic palace or even that old. On the plus side, the location is perfect: on a cliff edge with rooms overlooking the garden and sea and a lift that drops you right down on the beach. Some rooms have whirlpool baths and private patios. The restaurant is recommended, particularly the seafood; try the giant *langostinos*. There's also a pool and tennis court.

€€€ Balcón de Europa, Paseo Balcón de Europa 1, T952-520800, www.hotelbalconeuropa.com. With an unbeatable location right on the Balcón itself, this has bright and spacious rooms, decorated with elegant simplicity. The hotel is built in the rock face so the entrance is on the 6th floor (from the Balcón), while rooms have direct access to the private beach below. A good place to relax, with a piano bar, sauna and massage. Rooms with views and balcony cost some €30 more, but are memorable.

€€€ Hotel Carabeo, C Carabeo 34, T952-525444, www.hotelcarabeo.com. A delightful English-owned boutique hotel down a quiet side street near the centre. The furniture and decor throughout is sumptuous with tasteful antiques and paintings by acclaimed local artist, David Broadhead. There's a range of rooms (some are **€€**), including sea-view suites with great views and a private terrace. The elegant restaurant serves delicious modern Mediterranean cuisine and tapas. Recommended.

€€ Hotel Mena Plaza, Pl España, T952 520 965, www.hotelmena plaza.es. Excellent rooms for a very fair price are to be had at this central, modern hotel. Compact spotless rooms with contemporary decor are complemented by good service and a small pool. Location is great.

€€-€ Hostal Miguel, C Almirante Ferrándiz 31, T952-521523, www. hostalmiguel.com. A very appealing option on a pedestrian street near the Balcón de Europa, this renovated Andalucían townhouse offers good-value accommodation in bright and cheerful rooms with fridge and private bathroom. The owners are exceptionally helpful; there's also a lovely roof terrace with views – perfect for tasty breakfast or romantic sunset. Minimum 2-night stay in high summer. Recommended.

€ Mena, C El Barrio 15, T952-520541, www.hostalmena.es. A good location in the narrow backstreets west of the Balcón. The rooms in this friendly

10-room *hostal* are spotless, bright and cheery with interesting artwork. There's a pretty patio, and the best rooms have a balcony overlooking the clifftop garden for only €7 more. Recommended.

Camping
Nerja Camping, T952-529714, www.nerjacamping.com. Located around 5 km east of town on the N-340, the campsite is leafy and spacious, but the place gets busy in summer so book ahead. It's significantly cheaper off season but closes during Oct.

Restaurants

Nerja *p32*
There's a wide selection of restaurants to suit all pockets and tastes. Seafood restaurants are moderately priced here. Many restaurants close for part or all of the winter.

€€€ **Oliva**, C Pintada 7, T952 522 988, www.restauranteoliva. com. Stylish and popular, this is a reliable choice for upmarket but unpretentious dining. Plenty of thoughtful touches are allied with well-presented modern cuisine.

€€ **El Pulguilla**, C Almirante Ferrándiz 26, T952-523872. Typical of Málaga province with its no-nonsense stainless steel and tiles, this bar pulls in the crowds for its good-quality fried fish and other seafoody snacks. There's also ice-cold Cruzcampo beer, generous glasses of wine, and a free tapa with every drink.

€€ **La Marina**, Plaza de la Marina, T952-521299. Famous locally for its fish and seafood, cooked *a la plancha* (grilled), *hervido* (boiled), or *a la sal* (baked in salt). The cooking is simple yet uses the freshest ingredients.

€€ **Lan Sang**, C Málaga 12, T952-528053. This spot is an excellent and authentic Laotian restaurant with top-notch service, and attractive wooden tables. The food (all coded by spiciness and content) ranges from cracking fish curries to tasty vegetable stir-fries. Try the *khao niew* sticky rice, meant to be eaten balled up in your fingers.

€ **Esquina Paulina**, C Almirante Ferrándiz 45, T952-522181. An intimate, well-run and charming place, this offers quality wines, tasty gourmet tapas, fine *tablas* of ham or cheese, as well as coffee, cakes, and cocktails.

Bars and clubs

Nerja *p32*
Disco and karaoke bars cluster around Plaza Tutti Frutti (yes, that is its real name), just west of the main road, running down to the water. By night in summer, the **Papagayo** beachside restaurant turns up the volume with live music (from flamenco to hard rock) and DJs until sun-up.

Entertainment

Nerja *p32*
Flamenco
El Molino, C San José 4. Nightly show at 2100.

✳ Festivals

Nerja *p32*
Feb Carnaval for 3 days with parades and singing of *chirigotas* (popular songs).
16 Jul Fiesta de la Virgen del Carmen, the fishermen's fiesta; the statue of the Virgen del Carmen is carried down to the sea at Calahonda beach.
9-13 Oct Feria de Nerja, local saint's day and a week-long festival.

⊖ Transport

Nerja *p32*
There are buses more than hourly to **Málaga** (1 hr) and the coastal towns to the west; and several daily buses eastward to **Almuñécar**, **Granada** and **Almería**. Local buses head to and from the inland villages of the Axarquía, such as **Frigiliana**, **Torrox** and **Vélez Málaga**.

La Axarquía

This popular walkers' region was once notorious bandit country and later a guerrilla stronghold during and after the Civil War. Like the Alpujarra in Granada province, it preserves a distinctly North African character: the remains of the Moors' labours in creating terracing and irrigation channels can still be seen, while the small villages dotting the area are whitewashed, with narrow streets. The main settlement of the region, Vélez Málaga, isn't a particularly enticing place, as it is rapidly succumbing to overdevelopment fuelled by expat demand. The same is gradually happening to most of the villages – the only buildings not for sale are the estate agencies – but the region still has ample charms and offers some rewarding walking.

Driving through La Axarquía → *For listings, see pages 42-44.*

In an effort to encourage rural tourism, five routes have been devised for visiting La Axarquía by car, each colour coded and waymarked. Owing to the terrain, most of the routes are not circular and involve retracing one's steps in places, but they are, nevertheless, recommended. A detailed brochure describing the routes can be obtained from the tourist office in Nerja. Be prepared for some erratic signposting in the more remote parts of La Axarquía. The **Ruta del Sol y del Aguacat** (the Sun and Avocado Route) starts at Rincón de la Victoria and visits the agricultural villages of the Vélez valley, including Macharaviaya, Benamacarra and Iznate. The **Ruta del Sol y del Vino** (the Sun and Wine Route) starts in Nerja and includes the main wine-producing villages, such as Cómpeta and Frigiliana. The **Ruta Mudéjar** concentrates on architecture, looking at villages, such as Archez, Salares and Sedilla. The **Ruta de la Pasa** (the Route of the Raisin) looks at the more mountainous villages in the northwest of the area. Finally, the **Ruta del Aceite y los Montes** (the Route of the Oil and the Mountains) examines the olive-growing villages, such as Periana and Alaucín in the north of the area.

Tourist information
Vélez Málaga has no tourist office, so it's best to pick up information on the region from the offices in Nerja and Málaga before arriving. Alternatively,

there are small offices in the villages of Sayalonga, Cómpeta and Frigiliana (see below).

Vélez Málaga

The so-called capital of the Axarquía is only 4 km from the coast and is more of a gateway really, as it has little in common with the villages of the area apart from being steeply located on a hilltop. It wasn't reconquered by the Christians until 1487, and still preserves some of its Moorish fortress on a crag above the town. The parish church of **Santa María la Mayor** was built on the site of the main mosque, whose minaret has been converted into the belltower. There's a fine *mudéjar* ceiling inside.

Cómpeta and around

Despite the large numbers of northern European expats, this village is still one of the best spots to relax in the Axarquía. A wine-making village, the hills around are stocked with Moscatel grapes that are used to make a sweet wine. The main square is overlooked by the **Iglesia de la Asunción**. Nearby, on the main road, is a small **tourist office** ① *T952-553685, turismo@competa.es, Mon-Sat 1000-1500, Sun 1000-1400; this is also where the bus stops*. You can obtain local walking maps at the office.

Sayalonga and Archez

From the coast at Caleta de Vélez, a road snakes up into the hills towards Cómpeta via the typically picturesque villages of Sayalonga and Archez. The former has a **tourist office** ① *Pl Lorca 3, T952-535045, oficinadeturismo@sayalonga.es, May-Sep daily 0800-1400, 1600-1800, Oct-Apr 0830-1430*, which occupies the same building as a museum on morisco culture, with art, information on morisco life, and a run-down of the area's villages. Leave your car on the main road to explore the village, as you'd probably have to back it out again. The village's other main attraction is the **Cementerio Redondo**, which is indeed round. Sayalonga is also the start of a pleasant walk (see the Sayalonga circuit, below).

Not far beyond, and signposted left off the main road, **Archez** is another sleepy, pleasant village with a good place to stay and eat.

Frigiliana

Frigiliana, a mere 6 km from the coast and steeped in Muslim atmosphere, was the site of one of the last battles between the Christians and the Moors in 1569, and ceramic plaques record the events on the walls of the houses in the older part of the town. With narrow streets and whitewashed houses festooned with hanging plants and geraniums, it's perhaps the region's prettiest village, although also its most touristy. For the best view of the surrounding valley with its Mediterranean backdrop, climb up to the mirador with its handy bar and restaurant. The **tourist office** ① *Cuesta del Apero 10, Mon-Fri 0930-1900, Sat 0930-1400, 1600-2000, Sun 1000-1400, 1600-2000*, can provide information on accommodation.

Alfarnate

In the northwest of La Axarquía, not far from Antequera, is Alfarnate. On the road outside the village, the **Antigua Venta de Alfarnate** ① *Tue-Sun 1000-1800, T952 759 388*, claims to be the oldest inn in Andalucía. Once the haunt of assorted highwaymen and robbers, including the notorious El Tempranillo, it now houses a small outlaws' museum including a prison cell. The characterful *venta* serves excellent country food and is cheerfully crowded with Spanish families at weekends.

Walking in La Axarquía → *For listings, see pages 42-44.*

Getting around The best maps of the area are the standard 1:50,000 map of the Servicio Geográfico del Ejército, Series L. The walks described below are covered by maps: Zafarraya 18-43 and Vélez-Málaga 18-44. The Marco Polo bookstore in Cómpeta generally has both maps in stock.

What makes walking in La Axarquía such a treat is the very marked difference in climate, vegetation and terrain between the higher passes and the coastal fringe. The Mediterranean is often visible, sparkling in the distance, and on most of the walks the Sierra de Tejeda provides a spectacular backdrop, especially during the winter months when there is often snow on its higher reaches. Many walks in the area are waymarked.

Sayalonga circuit → *Distance: 10 km. Time: 3½-4 hrs. Difficulty: easy.*
This half-day excursion links two attractive villages, Sayalonga and sleepy Corombela. This walk begins in Sayalonga's Plaza Rafael Alcoba. Go past the Ayuntamiento into Calle Cristo, following signs for 'Cementerio Redondo'. Branch right along Calle Rodríguez de la Fuente, then, at the end, turn left. Pass a church to your left, then bear right downhill to a sign marking the beginning of the walk to Corombela. A dirt track leads downhill, passing beneath the cemetery, through fertile groves of fruit trees. The route is waymarked with white and yellow stripes. The track meets the river (15 minutes), runs beside it, then crosses it via a narrow bridge. With the river to your right, you soon pass the lovely Casa El Molino then begin climbing through lush, well-irrigated terraces. Not long after, the track changes course, heading away from the river up a side valley, past stands of bamboo and a cluster of farm buildings. Look for the *secaderos*, or drying platforms, used to dry the moscatel grapes. Continue

climbing and you pass another group of buildings to your left. You reach a fork (45 minutes). Ignore the track that branches right down towards a shed and rather go left and continue climbing. Cómpeta is now visible and Corombela comes into view.

The track runs past several small farms before descending slightly (one hour), crossing a gulley then passing Las Tres Fuentes, or the Three Springs, on your left. After passing a football pitch, the track meets a tarmac road. Go straight across into Corombela (one hour 20 minutes). Bear left just past the bakery to Bar Cantero, a good place for a drink after your long climb from Sayalonga. Here, swing left past a supermarket into Calle Las Pitas. Continue along a track that runs just above the Corombela/Daimalos road. The track climbs, passes Villa Alminara, then drops down to the tarmac road, which you should follow to the top of the pass. After 10 minutes of asphalt-bashing, where the road swings sharply right, turn left on a track (one hour 45 minutes), which leads past a farm where wine is for sale with more *secaderos*. At the next fork go right and soon you pass above four small farms. Follow the ridge along – on a clear day there are great views of the Sierra de Tejeda and La Maroma (2069 m) – past an ugly breeze-block building and, just before a modern house with arches, turn left following a track steeply downhill. Sayalonga is visible across the valley. You pass two pretty farms then a ruin on the right. Continue to descend, swinging sharply left and then right. Just before a ruined farm, branch right off the track, pass a few yards to the right of the ruin, then bear sharp right and drop down to a rough track which zigzags down towards a house with two palm trees, soon merging with a better track which arcs right towards the farm. Here go left and continue down and cross the river (two hours 15 minutes). You may need to remove boots in the wetter months. On the other side, bear right and, after 100 m, just past a lemon and an orange tree to the left of the track, branch left on a path which winds steeply up through the terraces. It is quite overgrown in parts. Where it becomes less distinct, swing left along the top of a vineyard, then drop down to a dirt track, then bear right and follow a rather messy track up to a breeze-block building. Passing to its left then climbing, you return to the sign marking the beginning of the walk. From here, retrace your footsteps back to Plaza Rafael Alcoba. **Map**: 1:50,000 Vélez-Málaga (1054).

Canillas de Albaida circuit → *Distance: 11 km. Time: 4½-5 hrs. Difficulty: medium.*
This enchanting walk takes you out from Canillas de Albaida via a beautiful riverside path, which meanders through thick stands of oleander, crossing back and forth across the Cájula river – easily passable unless there has been heavy rainfall. After a steep climb the middle section of the walk takes you along dirt tracks and is quite different in feel. But it is easy to follow and there are fine views of the Sierra de Tejeda. The final section of the walk – there is a

steep climb last thing – is along an ancient cobbled path with gorgeous views of Canillas and the Chapel of Santa Ana. Try to do this walk when the oleander is in flower for a real spectacle. There are some prickly plants on the middle section before you reach the forestry track, so you should wear trousers. **Map**: 1:50,000 Zafarraya (1040).

Itinerary The walk begins from the car park at the entrance of Canillas as you come from Cómpeta. Go down the hill from the roundabout past the supermarket and chemist. At the bottom, bear left at a sign for 'Finca El Cerrillo'. Head down past the chapel of San Antón, then bear right and drop down; cross the river, then immediately bear right following a concrete road towards an old mill. The road narrows to a path that runs beside the Cájula river, crossing back and forth several times. Pass a breeze-block building (20 minutes) on your left and continue along the river's right bank. You'll see red waymarking. Cross the river again and climb; there is beautiful old cobbling in places. After passing beneath an overhanging rock face, you descend back down to the river, cross it a couple more times, then the path climbs up the river's left bank between two fences and becomes a track. Ahead you will see a white farmhouse.

Be careful! Before you reach it, branch right (by a small orange tree to the left of the track) at a sign 'Camino del Río' along a narrow path that passes by a grove of young avocados. It winds past the stumps of a line of poplars, then continues on its rather serpentine course, occasionally marked by cairns. Shortly, your path is crossed by another, which has black water pipes following its course. Turn right here and then almost immediately left, then wind down to the river, which you cross via stepping stones. The path climbs up the other bank and soon becomes better defined (occasional red dots mark the way). Where the path divides, go left. A ruined house comes into sight on the other side of the river. Cross the river again and climb the path towards the house. You should pass just to the right of the house then climb steeply up the side of the valley. As you climb you'll see a solitary building on the crown of a hill. Remember this landmark – you'll pass by it later in the walk. The path swings right, descends, crosses a (dry) stream, then bears right again and winds uphill. You come to an area of terracing where you continue to climb. Above you to your right you'll see a small farmhouse. Head up to the farm, which you should pass just to its right. You reach a dirt track. Turn right here (one hour, 15 minutes) and head for the solitary building which you saw earlier in the walk. Just past the house, the track arcs left towards the head of the Cájula gorge and a small cluster of houses. The track winds, descends, crosses el Arroyo de Luchina via a concrete bridge with rusting railings, then climbs again past olive and citrus groves. After passing a house to your right, where a row of pines has been planted, you cross the river (one hour, 45 minutes). Continue past a row of poplars on the main track: don't turn sharp right on a track leading down towards the river. Follow this track, climbing at first, roughly parallel to the Río Cájula, heading back towards Canillas. Eventually you pass a water tank then a house to the right of the track with a solar panel (two hours). Just past this house, the track swings to the left and another track branches right (it has a chain across it). Ignore this turning, continue for 30 m and then – careful! – turn right away from the track on to a beautiful path that zigzags all the way down to the river Llanada de Turvilla. Somewhere to one side of the path would make a memorable picnic spot. Cross the bridge over the river then bear right and wind up towards the Santa Ana chapel. Pass beneath the chapel – the gorge is now down to your right – and, after a steep climb, the path becomes a track that leads you just beneath the cemetery, where a green mesh fence runs to your right. Bear sharp left past house No 35; go to the end of the street, then head up the hill past the supermarket and bank to arrive back at your point of departure.

La Axarquía listings

For hotel and restaurant price codes and other relevant information, see pages 6-12.

☺ Where to stay

There are many *casas rurales* in the Axarquía region. Check with local tourist offices, or online at www. andalucia.org, www.axarquiacosta delsol.es or www.toprural.com. There are also numerous villas, apartments and other holiday lets.

Cómpeta and around *p38*
€€ Hotel Alberdini, Pago la Lomilla 85, T952-516294, www.alberdini.com. Perched on a hill with wonderful views over the surrounding valleys, this rustic stone-clad rural hotel makes a relaxing base. Rooms are decorated in individual styles, and there's a restaurant, other good facilities and various activities like Pilates and Spanish classes. There are various free-standing bungalows, including one rather curious cave-like one. If coming from Sayalonga, turn right towards Torrox just before entering Cómpeta. Prices are very reasonable.
€€ Hotel Balcón de Cómpeta, C San Antonio 75, T952-553535, www.hotel-competa.com. With excellent facilities for the price, this neat and tidy hotel has good rooms with big beds, a terrace, pool, tennis court and restaurant. There are various types of room available.
€ Casa San Antonio, C San Antonio 6, T952-553517. Just above the central square on an attractive street, this offers solid, simple comfort at a fair price. There's 1 family room, with a sofa bed for the kids, and a bright spacious double. It's a good base for walkers, with laundry facilities.

Apartments

There are numerous houses for holiday rentals available in the village; ask at the tourist office or in one of the estate agents.

Casa La Piedra, at the top of the village, Plazoleta 17, T952-516329, www.competaholidayhome.com. This is a particularly good one.

Sayalonga and Archez *p38*

The tourist office in Sayalonga has details of a number of village houses for rent, either for a night or for a longer stay. Prices vary.

€€ Posada Mudéjar, C Alamos 6, Archez, T952-557854, www.archez turismo.com. This friendly option by the church in Archez has relaxing, colourful compact rooms with a Moorish touch.

Frigiliana *p38*

€€ Hotel Los Caracoles, Ctra Frigiliana-Torrox Km 4.6, T952-030068, www.hotelloscaracoles.com. One of the most unusually designed hotels in southern Spain, this has 5 striking bungalows (*caracoles*, or snails), that are romantic shell-shaped structures blending *modernista* architecture with North Africa via Greece and *Star Wars*. They are equipped with salon, bedroom and bathroom and have a double room and a sofa bed. There are also enchanting doubles with terrace, and a restaurant that has some Mozarabic-style dishes and cracking views over coast, hills, and villages. It's 5 km west of Frigiliana.

€€ La Posada Morisca, Ctra Frigiliana–Torrox Km 2, T952-534151, www.laposadamorisca.com. A couple of kilometres west of Frigiliana, this is an enchanting spot, and utterly relaxing. All rooms have views of the coast from their balconies, and elegant rustic-style decor. They also have wood-burning stoves and decent bathrooms. There's a good restaurant (dinner only) and a small pool.

€ Las Chinas, Plaza Capitán Conés, T952-533073, hotel-laschinas@terra.es. One of the best and longest-established of the smaller hotels, which has 9 rooms, slightly old fashioned but clean, comfortable and colourful, and a very good restaurant.

❷ Restaurants

See also the hotels for good eating options.

Cómpeta and around *p38*

€€ Museo del Vino, Av Constitución s/n, T952-553314, www.museodelvino competa.com. This isn't a museum but a shop. It deals out generous glasses of local wine, which you can accompany with traditional tapas of ham, chorizo or cheese. There's also a restaurant serving classy roast meats. It's a little tacky, but the food and service is good.

€€ Restaurante El Pilón, C Laberinto s/n, T952-553512, www.restaurantel pilon.com. Mon and Wed-Sat dinner, Sun lunch. On a steep street below C San Antonio, this Brit-run restaurant has an upstairs terrace and dining rooms with great views over the village and the hills beyond. It's warm and busy. Book ahead in summer.

✿ Festivals

Cómpeta and around *p38*
15 Aug Enjoy the local wine at the boisterous **Noche del Vino** festival.

Frigiliana *p38*
20 Jan Fiesta San Sebastián sees villagers walk barefoot through the streets carrying candles and the statue of San Sebastián.
Aug Annual **dance and music festival**, with plenty of *fino* and fiesta spirit.

⊖ Transport

Vélez Málaga *p38*
There are several daily buses from **Málaga** and frequent connections from **Torre del Mar** and **Nerja** on the coast.

Cómpeta and around *p38*
There are 3 daily buses to Cómpeta from **Málaga** via **Vélez Málaga**.

Frigiliana *p38*
Regular buses run from Torrox to Frigiliana.

Costa del Sol

The Costa del Sol is a curious mix of paradise and hell, a stretch of ribbon-developed coast where sun-blessed retirees rub shoulders with corrupt mayors and mafiosos looking for the next dodgy property deal. To impoverished Franco-era Spain the influx of tourists was a blessing; now, with competition from other holiday destinations in the Mediterranean and Caribbean, the concrete jungles can seem more of a curse, and the lack of foresight in approval of developments, not to mention the bribes taken to rubber-stamp them, is staggering.

Nevertheless, despite the timeshares and the crimes against architecture, it remains a good-time zone. Spain's former property boom meant that facilities improved, and it's not just a spot for cheap beer and a lobster tan. The ever-increasing numbers of 'residential tourists', generally middle-aged northern Europeans looking to live out their retirement years with a bit of decent sunshine has boosted the local economy and meant that the seaside towns aren't so reliant on the whims of the sun-seeking package tourist. While not even the Costa del Sol's biggest fan could describe the beaches as anything more than gritty, nor the cultural attractions anything more than token, the climate remains exceptional, and the ambience cheery. Still, it can seem like the least Spanish of places, with northern European languages dominant.

Torremolinos

Once a byword for all the worst aspects of Mediterranean tourism, Torremolinos has long been surpassed in crassness by other destinations and, if visited off season, can actually be quite pleasant. It is difficult to appreciate that 40 years ago there were hardly any buildings here, apart from the water mills that gave Torremolinos its name (and which stopped working in 1924) and a few fishermen's cottages behind La Carihuela beach. The centre of the former village is Calle San Miguel, now a busy pedestrianized alley full of boutiques, restaurants and a Moorish tower. Torremolinos has four beaches; for the best sand, atmosphere and restaurants head for La Carihuela, the old fishermen's quarter, with the most appealing part of the maritime promenade. There are three **tourist offices** ① *one at Bajondillo beach, Plaza de las Comunidades Autónomas s/n, T952-371909, one in La Carihuela, C Delfines 1, T952-372956, and one in the centre on Plaza Independencia, T952-374231.*

Benalmádena

Torremolinos merges imperceptibly into Benalmádena to the west. The name applies to both the pretty *pueblo*, 300 m above sea level, and the beachside development. The beach is one of the Costa's best, and there's an attractive marina where various companies offer boat trips out into the Mediterranean. There are also a couple of family-friendly attractions. Within the marina is **Sea Life** ① *T952-560150, www.visitsealife.com, daily 1000-1800, to 2000 May-Jun and Sep-Oct, to midnight Jul-Aug, €15.50, children €13.50*, a submarine park with plastic tunnels taking you into the aquarium for eyeball-to-eyeball contact with sharks, jellyfish and other sea creatures. It's substantially cheaper to book via their website. While travelling along the N340 you'll see the **Teleférico de Benalmádena** ① *T902-190482, www.telefericobenalmadena.com, return trips 1100 until dusk plus night trips Jul-Aug, closed Jan-early Mar, €7.40/€13.25 single/return*, a cable car swinging above the road to the top of the Calamorro mountain, 769 m above sea level. The journey takes 15 minutes and there are fantastic views; you can even spot Morocco on a clear day. Hikers can enjoy a choice of several trails when they reach the top. Alternatively, there's a bar, donkey rides and regular bird-of-prey displays.

Fuengirola

Fuengirola, a mere 20-minute drive from Málaga airport, is both a lively resort and a genuine Spanish working town, with a thriving fish dock and light industry in the suburbs to the north. It appeals to northern European retirees in the winter, when it feels fairly staid, and attracts large numbers of Spaniards in the summer, when it doesn't. The main **tourist office** ① *Av Jesús*

Rein 6, T952-467457, www.visitafuengirola.com, Mon-Fri 0930-1400, 1630-1900 (2000 in summer), Sat 1000-1300, at the old railway station, can provide maps and information.

Unlike Torremolinos, Fuengirola has a long history. Extensive Roman remains have been excavated; it was they who probably built the first structure at the **Castillo de Sohail** located on a hill by the river at the west end of the town. The castle was destroyed in 1485 in the Christian reconquest of the area, the Moors surrendering on the day of San Cayetano, the patron saint of Fuengirola today. In 1730, the castle was rebuilt to defend the coast against the British who had taken Gibraltar in 1704. During the Peninsular War in 1810, a British expedition of 800 men under General Blayney landed at the castle and advanced on Mijas, but later they retreated to the castle, where, humiliatingly they were obliged to surrender to 150 Polish mercenaries. At this time the population of Fuengirola was a mere 60 people; today, it is closer to 80,000. The Castillo de Sohail is now an outdoor auditorium where concerts take place. There is also a small exhibition centre/museum.

The small zoo, **Bioparc Fuengirola** ① *Av José Cela 6, T952-666301, www. bioparcfuengirola.es, daily 1000 until dusk, to midnight in Jul-Aug, €17.90, children €12.50*, is an excellent example of humane treatment. There are no cages, and four different habitats create a natural environment for the animals. The zoo is also heavily involved in conservation programmes and focuses particularly on African and Asian rainforest species. There are regular shows and events for children.

Mijas

This village is geared to the tourist (foreign residents outnumber Spaniards by two to one in the Mijas administrative district), with donkey rides, garish souvenirs and English-run restaurants. Despite all this, Mijas has a certain charm and is worth a visit. It has a long history, going back to Roman times, while the Moors built the defensive walls that partially remain today. The village is located 425 m above sea level at the foot of steep mountains. The *vista panorámica* in well-kept gardens above the cliffs gives superb views along the coast. There's a **tourist office** ① *Plaza Virgen de la Peña s/n, T952-589034, www.mijas-digital.es, Mon-Fri 0900-1800 (2000 summer), Sat-Sun 0900-1400*.

Housed in the former town hall, the **Mijas Museum** ① *Plaza de la Libertad s/n, daily 1000-1400, 1600-1900 (1700-2000 summer), free*, has various themed rooms, such as an old-fashioned *bodega* and bakery, and regular exhibitions are held in the gallery upstairs.

Donkey 'taxis' are popular in Mijas, and standard rates are €10 for a ride, or €15 to be pulled in a donkey cart.

In Spain, the name Marbella conjures up a host of images. As the place where many of the country's celebrities spend summer, it has glamorous connotations; Spain's tabloid press relocates here in August to keep track of A-listers hanging out in the latest glitzy nightclub. But Spaniards always knew there was plenty of sleaze behind the diamanté façade – Jesús Gil y Gil, an infinitely corrupt man, was mayor here for years; after his death, the police investigation Operación Malaya opened a stinking can of worms, centred around cash-for-development approval scandals and money-laundering.

Nevertheless, Marbella is still by far the most appealing of the Costa del Sol towns, if you stay in its picturesque old city or on the beach below. Here, there are excellent places to stay and eat, and a lively atmosphere all year. West of the centre, however, a hideous strip of pleasure palaces, plastic surgery clinics, and Ferrari repair shops line the road to Puerto Banús, a luxury marina and hubristic exercise in the poorest of taste. Cracking summer nightlife yes – but it's a depressing triumph of style over substance and reeks of Eastern European mafias and local corruption.

Arriving in Marbella

Getting there   The nearest airports are Málaga and Gibraltar, both accessible by road in under an hour. The nearest train stations are Algeciras to the west and Fuengirola to the east. There is a Málaga airport bus that leaves from Marbella bus station 10 times daily between 0530 and 2200.

Tourist information The main tourist office ⓘ *T952-771442, www. marbellaexclusive.com, Glorieta de la Fontanilla s/n, Mon-Fri 0900-2100 (0830-2030 winter), Sat 1000-1400*, is on the main promenade and is helpful. There's another **turismo** ⓘ *C Salinas 4, T952-761197, Mon-Fri 0830-2000 (2030 summer), Sat 1000-1400*, in the old town, with town maps.

Background

Marbella has a long history, having been populated at various times by Phoenicians, Visigoths and Romans, as well as being the most important Moorish town between Málaga and Gibraltar. Historians suggest that Moorish Marbella was a fortified town by the time it was taken by the Christians in 1485; they set about remodelling the layout of the fortress, but much of the Moorish street plan remains today.

The changes began in the mid-1950s when a Spanish nobleman named Ricardo Soriano introduced his friends to the area. His nephew, Prince Alfonso von Hohenlohe, built the **Marbella Club**, attracting a wealthy international set to the area. Marbella's inhabitants today include Arab royalty, stars of the media, famous sportspeople and members of Russian mafias. A visitor to Marbella might be surprised at its reputation, as life seems entirely normal on the surface, but the glitzy social life is there going on behind closed doors in luxury yachts, palatial villas and private clubs.

Marbella

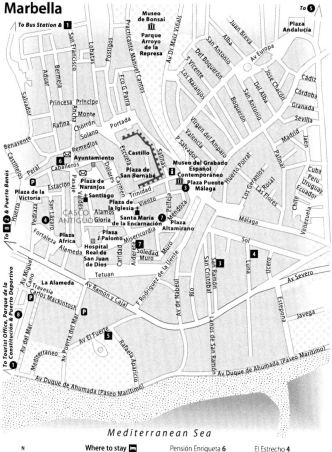

Mediterranean Sea

Where to stay	Pensión Enriqueta 6	El Estrecho 4
Albergue Juvenil 1	Town House 7	La Meridiana 2
Central 3		La Venencia 8
El Fuerte 5	Restaurants	Santiago 1
La Luna 4	Bar Altamirano 7	Ventas 5
Marbella Club 8	Bar El Cordobés 3	

Former mayor Jesús Gil actively promoted Marbella as a sort of Spanish Montecarlo, but ran up huge debts and was staggeringly corrupt. He had friends in high places but, once he died in 2004, his lackeys and co-conspirators found themselves in an exposed position. During the police investigation, Operación Malaya, some three billion euros in cash and valuables – paid for by illegally appropriated public funds – were seized, and over a hundred notables were arrested. These included the late Gil's protégé, Julián Muñoz, and Muñoz's lover, the famous *copla* singer and darling of the celebrity pages, Isabel Pantoja.

Places in Marbella

Marbella's **Casco Antiguo** (Old Town) is a compact area located to the north of Avenida Ramón y Cajal. In its centre is the pretty **Plaza de Naranjos**, opened up in the 16th century by the Christian town planners who demolished the maze of alleyways that comprised the Moorish *médina*. On the north side of the square is the 16th-century **Ayuntamiento** (town hall). In the southwest corner of the square is a delightful stone fountain, the **Fuente de la Plaza**, which dates from 1604. Nearby is the **Ermita de Nuestro Señor Santiago**, Marbella's oldest church, a small and simple building thought to date from the late 15th century. Look also for the **Casa Consistorial**, built in 1572. It has a fine wrought-iron balcony and *mudéjar* entrance, while on its exterior stonework is a coat of arms and inscriptions commemorating the bringing of water to the town. Finally in the square is the **Casa del Corregidor**, with a 16th-century stone façade, now a café.

Head for the northeast corner, particularly around Calle Trinidad, where there are good stretches of the old Moorish walls, and at the western end of this street stands one of the towers of the original **castillo**, built by the Moors in the ninth century. The old walls continue into Calle Carmen and Calle Salinas. Also at the east end of the old town, in Calle Misericordia, is **Hospital Real de San Juan de Dios**, which was founded by the Reyes Católicos at the time of the Reconquest to minister to foreign patients. It has a chapel with a panelled *mudéjar* ceiling and a tiny cloister.

The **Museo del Grabado Español Contemporáneo** ⓘ *C Hospital Bazán s/n, T952-765741, www.museodelgrabado.es, Mon 1000-1400, Tue-Fri 1000-1430, 1700-2030 (summer 1000-1400, 1800-2200), Sat 1000-1400, €3, under 18s free,* an exhibition of contemporary Spanish prints, is housed in the sympathetically restored **Palacio de Bazán**. This Renaissance building with an attractive exterior of pink stone and brickwork was originally bequeathed by its owner, Don Alonso de Bazán, to be a local hospital.

The **Museo Ralli** ⓘ *CN-340, Km 176, T952-857923, www.rallimuseums.com, Tue-Sat 1000-1400, closed mid-Dec to mid-Jan, free,* located in the Coral Beach complex a few kilometres to the west of Marbella, is a light and airy collection of fine Latin-American art and sculptures, as well as some paintings and graphic designs by Picasso, Dalí, Miró and Chagall.

Ojén

Just 8 km north of Marbella is the expanding village of Ojén, which has a history going back to Roman times. A number of springs rise in the village and this attracted the Moors who were in power here until 1570, and Ojén still retains much of the flavour of that time. It was once famous for the production of *aguardiente*, a powerful *anís*, but its main claim to fame today is the annual **Fiesta de Flamenco** during the first week in August. Ojén also has an interesting parish church that was built on the site of a mosque.

Continue through Ojén and over the pass and, after 4 km, turn left through the pine forests to the Refugio de Juanar and a walking track that leads through woodland of sweet chestnut, almonds and olives to a mirador at 1000 m, from where there are stupendous views over Marbella, the coast and, on clear days, Morocco. Allow 1½ hours for this walk. The wildlife is incredible, with a wide range of flowers, including orchids, butterflies and birds. Small family groups of ibex are not uncommon; during the spring and autumn, migratory birds of prey can be seen en route to and from the Straits of Gibraltar, while booted and Bonelli's eagles breed in the vicinity. The area can be crowded with picnickers on Sundays.

Estepona

Perhaps the most low-key and relaxed of the Costa del Sol resort towns, likeable and family-friendly Estepona has a long seafront backing a clean shingle beach. It's a quiet place, more a home for the grey diaspora than young funseekers, but has a few picturesque corners. It has an enthusiastic **tourist office** ① *Pl de las Flores s/n, T952-802002, turismo@estepona.es, Mon-Fri 0900-1800, Sat and Sun 0900-1400.*

Outside of town, north of the motorway, **Selwo Aventura** ① *Autovía Costa del Sol Km 162.5, T902 190 482, www.selwo.es, mid-Feb to Oct daily 1000-dusk, Nov Sat-Sun 1000-dusk, €24.50 for over-9s*, is a popular safari park where you can see various 'respect' animals from a truck that takes you around the complex. There are also various activities on offer. You can get significant discounts by booking ahead on their website.

Casares

Some 3 km west of Estepona, a winding road leads inland for 18 km to Casares, a lovely white town that attracts many tourists. Its whitewashed houses clothe the side of a hill which is capped by the ruins of a 13th-century **Moorish fortress** on Roman foundations, which was built in the time of Ibn al Jatib. The fort was also a centre of resistance against the French during the Peninsular War. Next to the fort is the **Iglesia de la Encarnación**, built in 1505 and with a brick *mudéjar* tower. There are majestic views from here along the whole coast and, on a good day, across to North Africa.

Casares is said to have derived its name from Julius Caesar, who may have been cured of his liver complaints by the sulphur springs at nearby Manilva. The 17th-century **Iglesia de San Sebastián**, which can be visited on the way to the fortress, is a simple whitewashed 17th-century building containing the image of the Virgen del Rosario del Campo. In the adjacent square is a statue of Blas Infante who was a native of Casares and leader of the Andalucían nationalist movement. He was executed by Falangists shortly after the start of the Civil War. The **tourist office** ⓘ *C Carreras 46, T952-895521, Mon-Sat 1000-1400, 1600-1900, Sun 1000-1400*, is located in the house where he was born, on the main road through town. They can provide details of a number of good circular walks that start from the main road just above the village.

From Casares, it is an exciting 20-minute drive to **Gaucín**, see page 76.

Costa del Sol listings

For hotel and restaurant price codes and other relevant information, see pages 6-12.

⊜ Where to stay

Torremolinos *p46*
There are plenty of rooms except at the height of the season. Most large package tour hotels are behind the eastern beaches; you get better rates for these booking through agencies. The best place to be based is La Carihuela.

€€€€ Hotel Amaragua, C Los Nidos 3, T952-384700, www.amaragua.com. In La Carihuela near Benalmádena marina, this is a sizeable and striking seafront hotel, with plenty of space, decent rooms, all with balcony, most with sea views (although these can be noisy). The location is good, and it feels more Spanish than British. There's a pool and spa, and standard 4-star facilities. 4-day minimum stay in season.

€€ Hotel Cabello, C Chiriva 28, T952-384505, www.hotelcabello.com. This small family-run hotel is a block back from La Carihuela beach. Rooms are clean and simply furnished; most have a sea view. There is a small bar with an adjacent small lounge with a pool table. Good value, especially outside of Aug, when it's **€**.

Fuengirola *p46*
Many hotels have reduced rates in winter.

€€ Las Islas, C Canela 12, Fuengirola, T952 375 598, www.lasislas.info. Easter-Oct. Unpromisingly set in the narrow lanes of the Torreblanca urbanization, this romantic hotel is quite a surprise with its relaxing tropical vegetation, sizeable pool and colourful, comfortable rooms with views. The onsite restaurant does some Lebanese dishes among other fare.

Camping

There are numerous sites close to the sea to the west of Fuengirola.
Fuengirola, Ctra Nacional 340, Km 207, T952-474108, www.camping fuengirola.net. 2 km from Fuengirola and a short walk from the beach, this has bar, restaurant, games area and a summer pool.

Mijas p47

The Mijas area has plenty of hotels.
€€ El Escudo de Mijas, C Trocha de los Pescadores 7, T952 591 100, www.el-escudo.com. Spotless, attractive rooms in a friendly location in the heart of Mijas pueblo.
€ Hostal Mijas, Plaza Virgen de la Peña, T952-486591. This no-frills spot offers simple but adequate accommodation in clean rooms with or without bath. Ask to see a few, as some have more light than others. Good value off season.

Marbella p48, map p49

Most of Marbella's hotels are on the outskirts. There's good budget accommodation within the old town itself.
€€€€ Hotel El Fuerte, Av El Fuerte, T902-343410, www.fuertehoteles.com. One of the few hotels in the centre, this is a charming older building dating back to the 1950s and renovated recently. Most rooms have balconies with sea views (substantially more expensive) and the furnishings are traditional with plenty of dark

wood. There is a lovely palm-filled garden with a pool situated between the hotel and the beach, just a few paces away. Recommended.
€€€€ Marbella Club Hotel, Bulevar Príncipe Alfonso von Hohenlohe s/n, T952-822211, www.marbellaclub.com. The **Marbella Club** opened its doors almost 60 years ago and has since become part of the Marbella tradition. The level of luxury is exemplary and facilities include a golf resort and riding stables, thalassotherapy spa and exclusive hair salon. The rooms, however, don't always live up to the hype, and you might be better off in one of the villas, which have their own garden area. There's also a smart restaurant, pool, gym, and a host of other 4-star facilities. You may get better rates from a travel agent.
€€€ The Town House, C Alderete 7, T952-901791, www.townhouse.nu. An appealing boutique B&B in a great location in the old town. It's very elegant, with white walls and furnishings offset by works of art. The rooms vary substantially; some are cosy, some more spacious. Best of all is the relaxing roof terrace – a quiet drink after a day at the beach goes down a treat here. Breakfast is included. Recommended.
€€ Hotel Central, C San Ramón 15, T952-902442, www.hotelcentral marbella.com. This has a superb location on a pretty flower-flanked pedestrian street in the old town. The rooms are cheery, with chessboard tiles, and small balconies; go for one overlooking the patio garden. All have a/c and free Wi-Fi access; there's also

a cosy sitting room with fireplace furnished with antiques. Prices are very reasonable.

€€ La Luna, C La Luna 7, T952-825778, hostallaluna.wordpress.com. The rooms here are situated around a central terrace. There are fans and fridges and the rooms are a good size and squeaky clean – so much so that owner Salvador will refund your money if you find so much as a speck of dust! Peaceful and friendly. There are several other good budget options in these narrow pedestrian streets east of the centre if it's full.

€€ Pensión Enriqueta, C Los Caballeros 18, T952-827552, www.hostalenriqueta.com. Close to Plaza los Naranjos, this has spacious, clean, good-value rooms with bathroom and friendly management. It's particularly well priced off season. You can put the car in the underground public car park right by the *hostal*. Recommended.

€ Albergue Juvenil, C Trapiche 2, T951-270301, www.inturjoven.com. Andalucía's best official youth hostel is just above the old town, and is a great, spacious facility with the bonus of a pool (summer only). Rooms vary in size, but are clean and modern; there's also disabled access, and a more-than-decent kitchen. Recommended.

Camping

There are a few excellent campsites near Marbella, all on the coast road, close to the beach. All are open year round. Booking is advisable Jul and Aug and during fiesta time.

La Buganvilla, Ctra N340, Km 188, T952-831973, www.camping buganvilla.com. Top category, bar, restaurant, laundry, beach, pool, watersports, golf, riding and tennis. There are also bungalows and 'bengalis', a cross between a tent and a cabin that go for about €45 in summer.

Around Marbella *p51*

€€€ Amanhavis Hotel, C Pilar 3, Benahavís, T952-856026, www.amanhavis.com. This hotel is a real one-off. The rooms are themed, ranging from a Moorish sultan's bedchamber to an astronomer's observatory. They vary substantially in facilities and price, but all are charmingly decorated. The restaurant here is excellent, specializing in fresh seasonal fare. Recommended.

Estepona *p51*

Book ahead for accommodation in Jul and Aug. There are numerous hotels, and you tend to get better rates via online hotel websites or travel agencies. Make sure you confirm the location; 'Estepona' can refer to a spot on the main road 5 km from town.

€ Hostal El Pilar, Plaza de las Flores 10, T952-800018, www.hostalelpilar.es. With a great location on the prettiest square in Estepona and a couple of mins from the beach, this offers plenty of value. Decoration is simple, airy, and cheerful, and the management are kindly. All rooms come with bathroom, and there are a few that sleep 4, good for families or groups.

Fuengirola p46

There is a vast and cosmopolitan range of choice in Fuengirola; however, the standard often leaves much to be desired. Head to C Capitán for a few more traditional eateries. Tapas bars are located mainly in the area to the west of the train station and on C San Rafael, which leads off the main square.

€€ **Bodega El Tostón**, C San Pancracio, T952 475 632, www. bodegaeltoston.com. A good tapas choice, decked out like a traditional Madrileño *bodega* with a vast selection of wine, served in enormous goblet-style glasses and accompanied by complimentary canapés or more filling fare.

€€ **Bodega La Solera**, C Capitán 13, T952-467708. Has barrel tables and walls lined with vintage wines. Tapas here include classy canapés like roquefort and dates and fuller meals are delicious, with excellent meats.

€€ **Mesón Salamanca**, C Capitán 1, T952-473888. A reliable option for good solid Castilian cuisine just off the main square on a street with several decent choices. It's traditional in feel and generous in portion.

Mijas p47

Mijas village has some excellent restaurants in among the 'chips with everything' establishments catering for the day trippers. If you head for the Plaza de la Constitución, there are several restaurants with stunning views down to the coast.

€€€ **El Padrastro**, Paseo de Compás, T952-485000, www.elpadrastro.com. Perched high on a cliff with access via lift or stairs, the views are magnificent and the dishes reflect an innovative twist on traditional fare. Try the *medallones de cerdo con pasas y piñones* (pork medallions with raisins and pine nuts in a Málaga wine sauce).

Marbella p48, map p49

There is a glittering array of eateries, including several of Andalucía's best.

€€€ **La Meridiana**, Camino de la Cruz, Las Lomas, T952-776190, www. lameridiana.es. Just west of town near the mosque with upbeat Moroccan-style decor and an enclosed patio for year-round alfresco dining. The menu includes roasts and fish dishes like *lubina grillé al tomillo fresco* (grilled sea bass with fresh thyme). Quality is trumped by high prices here, but the atmosphere can make it worth it for a romantic evening.

€€€ **Santiago**, Paseo Marítimo 5, T952-770078, www.restaurante santiago.com. Closed Nov. Appropriately located just across from the beach, this is a Marbella fish classic. The seafood here is catch-of-the-day-fresh with lobster salad a speciality. This is a popular restaurant with well-heeled locals, who wisely ask the professional staff for the day's recommendation. Meat dishes are also available, and the place also runs 2 tapas bars, 1 specializing in stews, around the corner. Highly recommended.

€€ **Bar Altamirano**, Plaza Altamirano 4, T952-824932, www.baraltamirano. es. Closed Wed. This buzzing place is vastly popular with locals and tourists alike, so get there early to bag your table and enjoy the well-priced *raciones* of rather tasty seafood and fish bought fresh from the market that morning. It's no-nonsense and traditional in feel and all the better for it. A real highlight is the warm and professional service.

€€ La Venencia, Av Miguel Cano 15, T952-857913, www.bodegasla venencia.com. In this promising tapas zone between the old town and the beach, this is the most outstanding choice. There's an excellent range of cold and hot plates; you can't really go wrong. There's cheerful seating around barrels both inside and out, and top service. Recommended.

€ Bar El Cordobés, C Arte 7, T952-829810. On the eastern side of the old town, just outside the walls, this simple spot is deservedly popular for its terrace, where typical Málaga fried fish is served. It's much less touristy than most, and has an authentic feel.

€ El Estrecho, C San Lázaro 12, T952-770004, www.barelestrecho.es. This reliable old tapas haunt is a well-established favourite on a narrow street off Plaza de la Victoria. It's full of locals enjoying the cheap and tasty morsels dished over the bar – the *albóndigas* and *ensaladilla rusa* stand out from the herd. Look out for the curious frieze depicting the social life of dogs. The **Bartolo**, opposite, specializes in fried fish and is also worthwhile.

€ Ventas, on the mountain road 3 km south of Ojén on the C337. For cheap food outdoors head for the 3 *ventas*,

which specialize in game dishes, especially rabbit and partridge.

Estepona *p51*
Apart from the big hotels outside town, the main restaurants are around pedestrianized C Real, a block back from the beach, and C Terraza, which crosses it in the centre.

€€ Restaurante Rafael, C Caridad 62, T952-808767. On the corner of C San Miguel, this smart contemporary spot is decorated with modern art and has affordable, imaginative cuisine.

Casares *p51*
€€ Bar Restaurant Claveles, C Arrabal s/n, T952-894095. On the square, this den of local bonhomie has its walls festooned with farming implements and specializes in game dishes such as rabbit, partridge and quail. Across the road, **Bar Los Amigos** is the throbbing heart of town and has great views from the terrace.

€€ Restaurante El Forjador, Ctra Casares Km 10, T952-895120, www. forgesrestaurant.com. Book ahead; opens for lunch Wed-Sun in winter and dinner Wed-Sat plus Sun lunch in summer. Just above the road between Estepona and Casares, this hideaway among larch and cork trees offers a warm welcome, views, and a sweet dining area and indoor terrace. Some British classics take their place on the menu alongside lamb curry, Moroccan chicken and Spanish-influenced plates. Leave room for dessert.

🎵 Bars and clubs

Marbella *p48, map p49*
Most of the action in the area takes place in Puerto Banús, rather than Marbella. From Marbella, buses run regularly from Av Ramón y Cajal just below the old town. **Sinatra's**, on the front line, is the most famous bar. In Marbella itself, most of the evening action is around Plaza Los Olivos at the top of C Peral in the old town, or in the port area, where there are a couple of dozen bars in a row.

✸ Festivals

Fuengirola *p46*
16 Jul Fiesta de la Virgen del Carmen. One of the best of its type along the coast. The statue of the Virgin is carried from the church in Los Boliches in a 2-hr procession to the beach and into the sea. An amazing spectacle, with half the inhabitants on the beach and the other half in the sea, either swimming or in boats.
First 2 weeks of Oct Feria del Rosario takes place on the showground site between Los Boliches and Fuengirola, where there are *casetas* for the various societies and brotherhoods. All this is accompanied by fireworks, bullfights and flamenco.

Marbella *p48, map p49*
Easter Semana Santa processions.
Jun Feria y Fiesta de San Bernabé celebrates Marbella's patron saint with concerts and firework displays.

Around Marbella *p51*
First week in Aug Fiesta de Flamenco, Ojén.

○ Shopping

Marbella *p48, map p49*
Good-quality shops abound in Marbella, particularly along Av Ricardo Soriano and in the alleyways of the old town. Many specialize in expensive jewellery and fashion goods. There are also numerous art galleries and craft shops.

♨ What to do

Marbella *p48, map p49*
Golf
Marbella is surrounded by golf courses, including **La Dama de la Noche**, T952-812352, www.golfdama denoche.es, the first floodlit course in Europe; **Río Real**, T952-779509, www.rioreal.com; **Aloha**, T952-812388, www.clubdegolfaloha.com; **Los Naranjos**, T952-815206, www.losnaranjos.com; **Las Brisas**, T952-810875, www.realclubdegolflasbrisas.es; **Guadalmina** (at San Pedro), T952-883375, www.guadalminagolf.com and **La Quinta** (road to Benahavís), T952-783462, www.laquintagolf.com.

⊖ Transport

Most of these bus services are run by **Portillo**, T902-143144, portillo.avanzabus.com.

Torremolinos and Fuengirola
p46

Regular buses run along the coast road between **Málaga** and Fuengirola (45 mins) via Torremolinos. There are also many services on to **Marbella** and a number of long-distance services from Fuengirola to other Andalucían cities as well as **Madrid**. Torremolinos is also a stop on the Fuengirola–Málaga railway, trains run every 30 mins in each direction.

Marbella *p48, map p49*

There are regular buses to and from **Málaga**, some express (50 mins), and some go via **Fuengirola** (45 mins) and **Torremolinos**. Heading west, there are regular buses to **Algeciras**, some via **Estepona**.

Other cities served include **Sevilla**, **Madrid**, **Granada**, **Ronda** and **Cádiz**. The main bus station is in C Trapiche, next to the bypass, but most local buses pass through the town centre.

Estepona *p51*

Estepona is served by regular daily buses along the coast in both directions.

Casares *p51*

The alternative route back to the coast at **Manilva** passes through attractive vineyards and limestone scenery, although the road surface is poor. There are 2 buses a day from **Estepona** to Casares.

North from Málaga

Málaga's hinterland, the province's most interesting zone, is a world away from the busy coast. The main town in the north of the province is Antequera, which has a host of interesting monuments as well as a range of natural attractions. While the most direct route north is via the N331 *autovía*, a more enticing option for those with transport sends you northwest via the El Chorro region, gouged with gorges and redolent with curious local history.

Garganta del Chorro

Taking the Cártama road from Málaga, continue along the course of the Río Guadalhorce to **Pizarra**, and then to the white hilltop town of **Alora**. A 14th-century Alcazaba stands above it, largely in ruins; it now serves as Alora's cemetery. On the town's main square is the huge parish church of La Encarnación, built in the 18th century and said to be the province's second largest place of worship after Málaga's cathedral.

Just north of Alora fork right and, after 12 km, you will arrive at Garganta del Chorro, or Desfiladero de los Gaitanes, a mighty but narrow ravine cut into the limestone by the Río Guadalhorce. The spectacular railway between Málaga and Bobadilla cuts in and out of tunnels along the side of the gorge, which in some places is over 300 m deep. Also following the side of the gorge is a narrow path, **El Camino del Rey**, which was built in the early 1920s and used by King Alfonso XIII when he opened the nearby hydroelectric works. The path today is closed and extremely dangerous, with large sections having fallen away. Search 'Camino del Rey' on YouTube for some interesting footage of the scary trail. There is a project underway to restore the Camino del Rey; it's projected to be ready to reopen around 2015, with a museum and other visitor facilities.

The gorge is a prime draw for rock climbers, who descend on El Chorro from all over Spain. There are many assisted climbing routes equipped with bolts or rings. Other activities you can arrange include canoeing and abseiling.

The hamlet of **El Chorro** is at the point the river is dammed, and it's where the train stops. It sits in spectacular surroundings; there's a hotel here, *casas rurales* nearby, and several hostels and campsites. It's also a popular lunch destination for *malagueños* at weekends.

Bobastro

Six kilometres north of El Chorro, Bobastro is what remains of the stronghold of one of the most interesting characters in the history of Al-Andalus. Ibn Hafsun was a *muwallad* (from a family of Christian converts to Islam) who became a renegade after killing a neighbour in AD 879. Fleeing to North Africa, he returned after a year and set himself up here, where he raised a ragtag army and became a real thorn in the side of the Córdoban rulers. Defeating various expeditions sent against him, he was captured in AD 883 and forced to join the army. After serving for a while, he deserted and returned to his fortress, where he rapidly started campaigning and conquering territory. At one point he held most of southern Andalucía with the help of various allies. He was never defeated and seems to have converted to Christianity; at any rate he built a church here. He died in AD 917, but his sons weren't able to keep hold of Bobastro for too long; it was retaken by Córdoba in AD 927.

Ibn Hafsun chose a wild, beautiful and highly defensible spot for his fortress, of which little remains atop the hill. Before reaching it, you pass the Mozarabic church in which later sources claim he was buried. It's a place of great beauty and solitude. It's in ruins, but a horseshoe arch has been preserved and the views are enchanting. Although Bobastro was once a sizeable town, scattered stones are all that remain.

Ardales and Carratraca

The main town in the region, Ardales is 10 km west of El Chorro. It's a typically pretty hilltop settlement, capped by a ruined castle that was presumably also built by Ibn Hafsun. Below it is the church, **Nuestra Señora de los Remedios**, which is a mixture of the *mudéjar* and Baroque; from the former style it conserves a fine wooden ceiling. Also in town are a couple of museums, one dedicated to the **Cueva de Ardales** ① *4 km outside of town, T952-458046*. Important Palaeolithic paintings decorate this cave, discovered in the early 19th century. The cave is closed to the public except by prior appointment, which you should arrange well in advance. If you read Spanish, the results of past geological and archaeological investigations are summarized on www.cuevadeardales.com.

Some 5 km southeast of Ardales is **Carratraca**, famous for its sulphurous waters, which were highly regarded back in Roman times. The village really took off in the 19th century when the despotic King Fernando VII built a mansion here for his personal use. Royal patronage made society sit up and take notice, and numerous famous visitors from all over Europe came here to take the waters, which, with a constant temperature of 18°C, is emphatically a summer-only pastime. There's a luxury spa hotel here, and in recent years, Carratraca has revived the performance of its ancient passion play, which takes place on Good Friday and Easter Saturday in the bullring, with a cast of over 100 villagers.

Antequera and around → *For listings, see pages 67-69.*

You know a town must be pretty old when even the Romans named it 'ancient place', or Antikaria. It's an excellent place to visit; on the city's edge stand three stunning prehistoric dolmens, perhaps the most impressive such monuments in Europe. The old town has numerous noble buildings of great interest, and the surrounding area offers tempting excursions to the dramatic rockscapes of El Torcal, the Lobo Park wolfery, and the flamingo lake of La Fuente de Piedra.

The dolmens are an obvious indication that the Antequera hilltop was an important prehistoric settlement, and the town's strategic position at the head of one of the easiest routes to the coast also appealed to the Romans. The Moors fortified the town with a citadel and, as part of the kingdom of Granada, Antequera didn't fall to the Christians until 1410. After becoming an important military base for assaults on the remaining Moorish possessions, the city grew in wealth in the 16th and 17th centuries, from which period most of its monuments date.

Places in Antequera

The centre of Antequera is Plaza San Sebastián, on which stands the **tourist office** ① *C Encarnación 1, T952-702505, turismo.antequera.es, Mon-Sat 0930-1900, Sun 1000-1400*, which has helpful information on the town and area.

At the top of town, the **Arco de los Gigantes**, a triumphal arch built in 1585, gives on to the attractive Plaza de los Escribanos, by which stands the town's most impressive church, **Real Colegiata de Santa María la Mayor** ① *Mon-Sat 1030-1730 (to 1900 summer), Sun 1030-1500, €3*, with a beautiful Renaissance façade worked on, among others, by the master Diego de Siloé in the mid-16th century. The spacious interior is now used for exhibitions and concerts and is a fine space with fat Ionic columns and a wooden ceiling. The cedarwood baldachin is a recent replica of the original. From the terrace beside the church, as well as stirring views, you can examine the excavated **Roman baths** below you.

The hillside above the church is covered with a peaceful hedged garden stretching up to the **Alcazaba** ① *opening as for Santa María la Mayor, €6 including Santa María la Mayor*, the remains of the Moorish fortress. The best-preserved feature is the **Torre del Homenaje** (keep) from the 13th century. The castle has been comprehensively restored (actually, completely rebuilt in places, which has raised various authenticity questions) and is an atmospheric spot. From the hilltop you look across to the curiously shaped hill known as the **Peña de los Enamorados** (Lovers' Hill), from which it is said that a pair of star-crossed Moorish lovers threw themselves when their union was prohibited.

Antequera's rich archaeological heritage is represented in the **Museo de la Ciudad de Antequera** ① *Plaza del Coso Viejo, Tue-Fri 0930-1400, 1630-1830, Sat 0930-1400, 1600-1900, Sun 1000-1400, €3*, near the Plaza San Sebastián. Set in a *palacio* dating from the Renaissance, it's a display of mixed quality, but has some outstanding pieces. The pride and joy of the museum is a famous Roman bronze statue dating from the first century AD. A life-sized depiction of a naked boy known as Efebo, it's a fine work. There are also some high-quality Roman mosaics in the museum. Another sculpture worth a look is a beautifully rendered St Francis, which is attributed to Alonso Cano.

There's another museum nearby, in the **Convento de las Carmelitas Descalzas** ① *Plaza de las Descalzas s/n, T606-855792, Tue-Fri 1030-1400, 1700-2000, Sat 0900-1230, 1700-2000, Sun 0900-1230, closed July, guided tours on the half hour, €3.30,* the order founded by Teresa of Avila. The visit is by guided tour and as worthwhile for the building as for the artworks, although a Luca Giordano depiction of Teresa herself is a fine work.

Antequera is full of other churches; in fact, although it likes to call itself the Athens of Andalucía, Rome might be (marginally) more accurate. Among them is the **Iglesia del Carmen** ① *Tue-Fri 1100-1330, 1630-1745, Sat-Sun 1100-1400, €2,* which has a *mudéjar* ceiling but is most notable for its excellent wooden *retablo*. Dating from the 18th century, it was carved by Antonio Primo in incredible size and detail; it's decorated with a wealth of scrolls, volutes and cherubs, as well as figures of popes, archbishops, John the Baptist and other prophets. Also look out for the pretty organ in the gallery and some ornate frescowork in one of the side chapels.

On the Plaza del Portichuelo, look out for the highly unusual arched brick façade of the small chapel, the **Tribuna del Portichuelo**. On the same square is the church of **Santa María de Jesús**, a bright white Baroque creation.

Dolmens
① *All dolmens Tue-Sat 0900-1830, Sun 1000-1700. Free.*
The highlight of any visit to Antequera will be a visit to these hugely impressive and moving monuments. They are megalithic in the true sense of the word, consisting of vast slabs of stone, the largest of which weighs a massive 180 tons. The stones were dragged over 1 km from a nearby quarry. After erecting the upright stones, earth ramps were constructed to manoeuvre the covering slabs into place. There are three dolmens, dating from the Chalcolithic period; they were built as burial chambers, presumably for important chiefs.

The adjacent **Menga** and **Viera** dolmens are about 1 km from the centre of town. From Plaza San Sebastián, walk down Calle Encarnación past the tourist office, carry on straight ahead, and follow the road (now Calle Carrera) left. Eventually you'll reach the entrance to the dolmen area on your left. You access the dolmens through an interpretation centre that provides some context. Menga, the oldest of them, dates from approximately 2500 BC, and is an eerily atmospheric chamber roofed with vast stone slabs. Recently, a deep well has been discovered at one end of the chamber. At the entrance, the staff on duty will point out the faint engravings in the portal. On Midsummer's Day, the rising sun shines directly into the chamber from behind the Peña de los Enamorados, clearly of ritual significance. The Viera dolmen dates from some five centuries later and has an access corridor leading to a smaller burial chamber.

El Romeral dolmen stands a further couple of kilometres out past the Menga and Viera dolmens; turn left when you reach the major intersection (head for Córdoba/Sevilla), then turn left after crossing the railway line. It dates to around 1800 BC and presents a very different aspect, with smaller corbelled stones being used to wall the access chamber and half-domed burial chamber, which is entered through a doorway.

El Torcal

This massive chunk of limestone, 16 km south of Antequera, has been weathered into rugged and surreal sculptural karstic formations and is a memorable place to visit, although preferably on a weekday when it's less crowded. The bulk of the massif is a *parque natural* and a **visitor centre** ① *T952-702505, daily 1000-1700 (1900 summer)*, atop it has exhibitions on the formations and wildlife; there's also an audiovisual presentation. From here, there's a short path leading to a stunning viewpoint and, from the centre's car park, two marked walking trails of approximately 45 minutes and two hours' duration. Spring is an excellent time to explore El Torcal, as the grey rocky zone is enlivened by a riot of colourful wildflowers.

The closest town is **Villanueva de la Concepción**, 18 km southwest of Antequera and served by buses from there and Málaga. The tourist office in Antequera can arrange a taxi to take you to the visitor centre, wait for you to do the trail, and take you back to town.

Lobo Park

① *Ctra Antequera–Alora Km 16, T952-031107, www.lobopark.com, Thu-Tue 1000-1800, tours 1100, 1300, 1500, 1630, €11, children €7.*

An intriguing spot to visit in easy striking distance of Antequera, this wolf park houses a variety of lupine residents rescued from the wild or captivity. The tour visits the enclosures of several different packs – Iberian, timber, European and Arctic wolves are all present. There's heaps of information – enquire ahead if you want an English-speaking guide – and it's fascinating to see the packs' strict hierarchies, plus the group 'bonding' behaviour after being fed. There's a good ecological vibe here, and the visit also includes a look at some domestic animals – a hit with the kids, but also great to see some animals rescued from the wild, including foxes who literally jump for joy when their handler approaches. A few nights a month from May to October you can pre-book a visit to hear the wolves howling in unison; an eerie moonlit sound. It includes dinner; check the website for dates.

The Alhambra

From Málaga, Granada's marvellous Alhambra is easily accessible on a day-trip or overnight visit.

Getting there

ALSA (www.alsa.es) runs hourly buses (1½-2 hours) from Málaga's bus station to Granada; this is a better option than the train, which requires a change in Antequera. By car, it's a 90-minute drive north via the A45 then east on the A92.

Tickets and opening hours

For details, see www.alhambrade granada.org. The complex is open daily, 0830-2000 from mid-March to mid-October, and 0830-1800 from mid-October to mid-March; last entry is one hour before closing and night visits are also available. Adults €13, under-12s free.

You'll be assigned either a morning ticket (up until 1400) or an afternoon ticket, and allocated a specific half-hour period during which you must enter the Palacios Nazaríes (see below), although you can stay there as long as you choose.

It's best to buy your ticket in advance at www.alhambra-tickets.es, or at La Caixa cash machines. If you just turn up at the ticket office, expect long queues; you may have to 'come back tomorrow' in busy periods.

History

Of all Spain's historical monuments, the Alhambra (from the Arabic *al-qalat al-hamra*, meaning the red fort) stands supreme. Among the final manifestations of Moorish culture in the peninsula, its history mirrors that of Spain in the succeeding six centuries. Taken by Fernando and Isabel in the Reconquest, it eventually fell into dereliction and was then used as a barracks in the war-torn 19th century. Rediscovered by Romantic travellers, it is now one of Europe's most-visited destinations.

The Alhambra as we see it today was principally a construction of the Nasrid dynasty, which rose to power in the 1230s and established it as their seat of power until their fall in 1492. After Boabdil surrendered the city and fortress to the Catholic Monarchs, many modifications were made to the existing structures, and several new edifices, including the Palacio de Carlos V, were built.

Palacios Nazaríes

The pinnacle of any Alhambra visit is the magical closed world of the Moorish palaces. Despite alterations, this ensemble is a staggering architectural and artistic achievement.

The palaces are entered through the **Mexuar**, which has several features that recur throughout the building. The ceramic dado decorated with coloured polygons is typical, as is the inlaid wooden ceiling and the arches with their *mocárabes* (stalactite work).

The decoration of each room follows the Islamic architectural principle of hierarchy. Small and intricate pieces of pattern join to form a larger design. A tiny tiled motif becomes a star in an entire firmament. The message is reinforced by the repetition of Arabic phrases and poems that describe the Alhambra as a small jewel reflecting the unimaginable grandeur of Allah.

The **Patio del Cuarto Dorado** is a small courtyard with a fountain, dominated by the high façade of the Salón de Comares. Beyond it, cramped corridors lead to the **Patio de los Arrayanes** (Court of the Myrtles), centred on a large pool of water. The surrounding chambers include the **Sala de la Barca**, named after the Arabic *baraka* (blessing) inscribed on the wall, and the **Salón de Comares**, surrounded by highly adorned alcoves and capped with a star-studded wooden ceiling.

The next courtyard is the much-photographed **Patio de los Leones** (Court of Lions) in which the grace of Moorish design reaches new heights. A fantasy of stonework frames the central fountain. Two pavilions supported by supremely delicate columns and arches face each other across the courtyard, which is framed by an elegant colonnade. On one side is the **Sala de los Abencerrajes**, graced by a cupola of *mocárabes*. At the far end is the **Sala de los Reyes**, featuring paintings on sheepskin, depicting Christian-influenced portraits and knightly scenes. The **Sala de Dos Hermanas** has another grand cupola, while the adjoining **Sala de los Ajimeces** has a dado of coloured tiles, stucco work and ceiling embedded with stained glass. It has perhaps the most romantic of the Alhambra's lookouts, the **Mirador de Lindaraja**.

Palacio de Carlos V

Many words have been written in prosecution and defence of this controversial building, but as a piece of Renaissance architecture, it has several striking features. Massive blocks of stone are studded with huge rings held in the mouths of lions and eagles. The circular central courtyard is an imposing space with superb acoustics; around it are an octagonal chapel, the **Museo de la Alhambra** and the **Museo de Bellas Artes**.

La Alcazaba

The fortress part of the compound is muscular, functional and highly impressive. Older than the rest of the buildings, its finer features were destroyed by Napoleon's troops in the Peninsular War. Its effective defensive design is immediately evident upon entering: you are forced to walk along a narrow passageway overlooked by high towers. The **Torre de la Vela** (watchtower) looms large over the city and has a spectacular panorama.

Generalife

This summer palace is reached via a grove of cypress and jasmine. Its central feature is the beautiful **Patio de la Acequía**, where an array of criss-crossing water jets sprinkle into a long pool. The belvedere, which gives fine views, was a Christian addition. At the end of the patio is the **Sala Regia**, or royal hall, accessed through a five-arched portico.

Laguna de la Fuente de Piedra

Twenty kilometres northwest of Antequera, this large saltwater lake is one of Europe's most important breeding grounds for the greater flamingo. The loveably awkward pinkish birds arrive early in the year to rear their chicks and hang around until the water level drops in summer, usually in late July or August. There are dozens of other waterbird species present, including avocets, terns and the rare white-headed duck. There's an **information centre** ① *T952-111715, 1000-1400, 1600-1800 (1800-2000 Apr-Sep)* by the lake that hires binoculars and provides birdwatching advice.

Nearby, **El Refugio del Burrito** ① *T952-031622, www.elrefugiodelburrito.com, 1100-1800 Oct-Mar, 1100-1900 Apr-Sep, free*, rescues donkeys and mules from across Europe and brings them here to rehabilitate and enjoy retirement in the Andalucían sunshine. It's great for kids and entry is free, but the organization relies on donations, so you may want to sponsor one of the gentle long-eared beasts for €15 per year.

Archidona

Some 15 km east of Antequera lies this once strategic town. Occupied by the Iberians, the Romans and the Moors and defended by a hilltop castle, it was captured by Christian forces in 1462. Later it was the chief town of the Counts of Ureña and the Dukes of Osuna.

Today, it is a backwater, bypassed by both the main road and the *autovía* to Granada. Its pride and joy, however, is Plaza Ochavada, a late 18th-century octagonal square, surrounded by buildings using ornamental brickwork and stone. It's a lovely space, and on it is the **tourist office** ① *T952-716479, www.archidona.org*. Further up the hill, a palm-shaded plaza is home to the Casa Consistorial, which boasts a beautiful carved façade. It now houses the municipal museum.

North from Málaga listings

For hotel and restaurant price codes and other relevant information, see pages 6-12.

Where to stay

Garganta del Chorro *p59*
There are several *refugios* near the train station charging around €10-15 for a dorm bed. There's also a campsite.

€€€ Cortijo Valverde, Apt 47, Alora, T952-112979, www.cortijovalverde. com. A rural hotel set in olive and almond groves near El Chorro. Each cottage has its own terrace and superb views. There's a pool, the hotel makes an environmental effort and walking and other activities in the area can be arranged. Breakfast is included, and other meals are available. Minimum 2-night stay.

€€ Complejo Turístico La Garganta, Bda El Chorro s/n, T952-495000, www.lagarganta.com. Dominating the hamlet, and offering spectacular views over the reservoir and gorge, this former flour mill is now a hotel. Attractive rooms and apartments are compact but fairly priced; it's more for a room with balcony. All have modern rustic decor; there's a pool, and the outdoor restaurant terrace buzzes with contented chatter during weekend lunches.

€ Finca La Campana, T626-963942, www.fincalacampana.com. A hospitable base run by climbers 2 km from the railway station. They offer climbing, caving and mountain-bike excursions and have cosy double and family accommodation in a variety of cottages or in the *refugio*, where a dorm bed costs €12. You can also camp. All guests have use of the kitchen, and there's a shop. Mountain bikes, climbing gear and kayaks can be hired here. Reception open 0900-1100, 1900-2100. Recommended.

Ardales and Carratraca *p60*
€€€€ Villa Padierna, C Antonio Rioboo 11, Carratraca, T952-489542, www.thermasdecarratraca.com. Easter-Oct. This luxury spa hotel seeks to recreate the glory days – Roman, Moorish and 19th century – of taking the waters. The installations are magnificently attractive, as is the building, but it's hard to feel the rooms offer value – try to nab a deal that includes spa treatments or meals.

€€ Posada del Conde, Pantano del Chorro 16-18, Ardales, T952-112411, www.hoteldelconde.com. This stately old building has been well converted into a comfortable hotel. It has high-quality rooms, with plenty of space and good bathrooms, and a restaurant serving generous and elaborate cuisine including hearty Castilian roasts.

€ Pensión El Cruce, Ctra Alora–Campillos s/n, Ardales, T952-459012. It's on the main road but has friendly management. It's a good deal, with a downstairs restaurant and spotless rooms with en suite bathroom and access to a balcony; there's also a pool.

Antequera and around *p61*

€€€ Parador de Antequera,
C García de Olmo s/n, T952-840901,
www.parador.es. The town's modern
parador is near the bullring on the
edge of town and offers quiet comfort.
There's a pool and pleasant gardens;
the rooms have polished floors
and large beds.

€€ Hotel Coso Viejo, C Encarnación
5, T952-705045, www.hotelcosoviejo.
es. This handily central hotel on the
museum square is modern in feel,
but preserves the building's original
features, including a beautiful patio.
The rooms are nothing special, but are
spacious and comfortable, if a little
dark. There's also a decent restaurant.

€ Hospedería Coso San Francisco,
C Calzada 31, T952-840014, www.coso
sanfrancisco.com. This excellent *hostal*
is in a beautifully restored old building.
The rooms are great value, with
attractive furnishings, heating, a/c, and
a bathroom. There's a patio restaurant
below, with occasional live music.

€ Hotel Plaza San Sebastián, Plaza
San Sebastián 4, T952-844239, www.
hotelplazasansebastian.com. Centrally
located, this friendly hotel has recently
renovated modern rooms with a/c,
heating and good bathrooms. A sound
choice lacking character but good value.

El Torcal *p63*
Camping
Camping El Torcal, on the way to El
Torcal, 6 km south of Antequera, T952-
111608, www.campingeltorcal.com.
Open all year with various bungalows
and apartments as well as tent and
van spots.

Laguna de la Fuente de Piedra
p66
Camping
Camping Fuente de Piedra, Camino
de la Rábita s/n, T952-735294, www.
camping-rural.com. A good base for
flamingo-watchers, this well-equipped
campsite is close to the lake and
open all year. As well as tent and van
sites, there are bungalows and rooms
available. Pool and bar/restaurant.

Restaurants

Ardales and Carratraca *p60*
On and around the central Plaza de
San Isidro, Ardales, are a handful of
good tapas bars, including **El Mellizo**,
and the excellent **El Casino**, a lively
local place with a variety of filling
snacks and *raciones*.

Antequera and around *p61*
€€ El Angelote, Plaza Coso del
Viejo s/n, T952-703465. A classy
place on the museum square,
specializing in generous portions of
local Antequera specialities such as
marinated partridge, *boquerones* (fresh
anchovies) stuffed with spinach and a
range of the town's famous desserts.
The lamb is also tasty, and there's a
decent *menú del día* for €12.

€€ Mesón El Escribano, Plaza de
los Escribanos 11, T952-706533. This
popular restaurant has a terrace
looking out at the collegiate church
and specializes in local dishes such as
porra, a thick tomato cold soup similar
to *salmorejo*. Reliably good.

🎵 Bars and clubs

Antequera and around *p61*
Manolo Bar, C Calzada 14, T952-841015. With a Wild West theme, it serves coffee, tapas and mixed drinks to a variety of Antequera folk in the mornings and late into the night.

⊖ Transport

Garganta del Chorro *p59*
There are no buses to El Chorro, but 1 train Mon-Sat arrives from **Málaga** (40 mins), currently leaving at 1840. It also stops in **Alora**. The train continues to **Ronda**.

Ardales and Carratraca *p60*
There are 4 daily buses from **Málaga** to Ardales; these continue to **Ronda**.

Antequera and around *p61*
Antequera is well served by buses from **Málaga**, which run almost hourly (1 hr) from the bus station, a 15-min walk north of Plaza San Sebastián. There are 5 daily buses to **Granada**, and 5 to **Sevilla** via **Osuna**. There are also connections to **Córdoba** and other Andalucían cities.

The train station is 1.5 km north of the town centre. There are 3 daily trains to **Ronda** (1 hr 10 mins) and services to **Sevilla** (4 a day, 1 hr 50 mins), **Granada** and **Algeciras**. Regular fast trains between Málaga and Córdoba stop at Antequera-Santa Ana station, 17 km west of town.

Laguna de la Fuente de Piedra *p66*
There are 3 buses daily from **Antequera** to Fuente de Piedra village.

Archidona *p66*
6-7 daily buses between **Antequera** and Archidona (20 mins), continuing to **Granada**.

Ronda

"There is one town that would be better than Aranjuez to see your first bullfight in if you were only going to see one and that is Ronda. That is where you should go if you ever go to Spain on a honeymoon or if you ever bolt with anyone." Ernest Hemingway, *Death in the Afternoon*.

The cradle of bullfighting as we know it, Ronda features high on the must-see list of many visitors to Andalucía because of its picturesque whitewashed streets and, most spectacularly, its position straddling a deep gorge that separates the old and new parts of town. The gorge is spanned by the Puente Nuevo, a late 18th-century bridge that crosses 80 m above the stream below. These attractions mean that it's overrun with tourists in peak season; to really appreciate the town you should spend a night or two here, as most people come on day trips and by six in the evening the tour buses have rolled back to the coast. Pack a thick coat if you plan to visit in winter.

Arriving in Ronda → *Phone code: 952.*

The largest of the white towns in these parts, Ronda sits atop a hill, which is cut in two, by a deep, narrow gorge, known as El Tajo, formed by the Río Guadalevín. The centre of town is Plaza de España on the edge of the ravine; from here the Puente Nuevo crosses the drop to the original Moorish part of town, where most of the interesting monuments are located. The larger Christian expansion, known as the Mercadillo, stretches north and east of Plaza de España and is the main focus for the daily life of *rondeños*; it's also where most of the restaurants and bars are located. Ronda's bus and train stations are both on Avenida de Andalucía on the northern edge of the new town, a 10- to 15-minute walk from Plaza de España. ▸▸ *See Transport, page 79.*

Tourist information Ronda has two tourist offices, both close together, and a useful tourism website, www.turismoderonda.es. There's the **Junta office** ⓘ *Plaza de España 1, T952-871272, Mon-Fri 0900-1930 (2000 in summer), Sat and Sun 0930-1500*, and the **municipal office** ⓘ *Plaza de Teniente Arce s/n, T952-187119, Mon-Fri 1000-1800, Sat 1000-1700, Sun 1000-1430*, next to the bullring. Both have a wide range of information in several languages on the town and area.

Background

In the collapse of the Córdoba caliphate, Ronda was seized by a Berber general and became its own *taifa* state before being annexed by Sevilla in 1066. Ronda wasn't reconquered by the Christians until 1485, when it was taken by forces under Fernando, the Catholic monarch. Always a centre for resistance and bandit activity, the Ronda area held out strongly in the 19th century against the invading French forces, leading villagers to chant 'Napoleón, Napoleón, conquistaste toda España, pero no pudiste entrar en la tierra de las castañas' (Napoleon, Napoleon, you conquered all of Spain, but you never could enter the land of the chestnuts).

Later, the town was popularized by Romantic travellers and became a haunt of artists and writers. Gustav Doré, Rainer Maria Rilke and Ernest Hemingway are among those who spent much time here. In the Civil War, many right-wingers were brutally murdered and the town shared its resources along a strict socialist system; reprisals after the Nationalist takeover were also fierce.

Places in Ronda → *For listings, see pages 76-79.*

Plaza de España and the Puente Nuevo

It's likely that you'll make this your first port of call in Ronda, as looking down into the gorge has a magnetic appeal. The plaza itself is dominated by the former town hall, now a *parador*. After pondering for a moment what idiot allowed a McDonald's to be opened next to it, move over to the Tajo and look down 80 m or so into the narrow gorge. The Puente Nuevo was built in the late 18th century and designed by José Martín de Aldehuela. Legend says that he died falling into the gorge while carving the date – the final act – on the bridge, but this is in fact untrue – he died in Málaga several years later. The stones were raised on pulleys from the bottom of the Tajo. Within the bridge itself is an **interpretation centre** ① *Plaza de España s/n, T649-965338, Mon-Fri 1000-1900 (1800 winter), Sat and Sun 1000-1500, €2,* in what used to be a small prison. Apart from the knowledge that you're standing over the ravine, there's little worthwhile here.

Plaza de Toros

① *C Virgen de la Paz s/n, T952-874132. Daily 1000-1800 (2000 in summer), €6.50, €8 with audioguide.*

One of the country's oldest, the Ronda bullring has a special appeal to lovers of tauromachy, for it was here that the rules for modern bullfighting were laid

Ronda

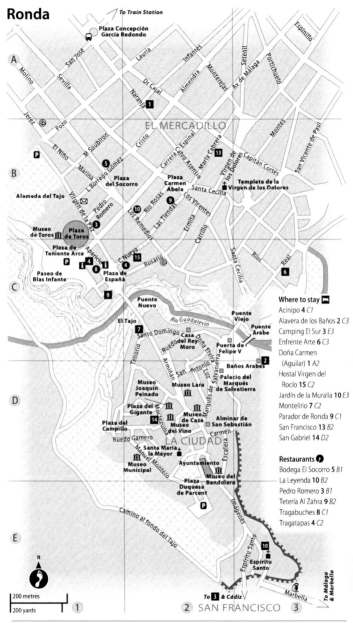

EL MERCADILLO

Plaza Concepción
García Redondo

To Train Station

Plaza del Socorro

Plaza Carmen Abela

Templete de la
Virgen de los Dolores

Alameda del Tajo

Museo de Toros

Plaza de Toros

Plaza de
Teniente Arce

Paseo de
Blas Infante

Plaza de
España

Puente
Nuevo

Puente
Viejo

Puente
Árabe

El Tajo

Río Guadalevín

Casa Don
del Rey
Moro

Puerta de
Felipe V

Baños Árabes

Museo
Joaquín
Peinado

Museo Lara

Palacio del
Marqués
de Salvatierra

Plaza del
Gigante

Museo
de Caza

Museo
del Vino

Alminar de
San Sebastián

LA CIUDAD

Plaza del
Campillo

Santa María
la Mayor

Museo
Municipal

Ayuntamiento

Museo del
Bandolero

Plaza
Duquesa
de Parcent

Camino al fondo del Tajo

Espíritu
Santo

To Málaga
& Marbella

To 3 & Cádiz

SAN FRANCISCO

N

200 metres

200 yards

Where to stay

Acinipo 4 C1
Alavera de los Baños 2 C3
Camping El Sur 3 E3
Enfrente Arte 6 C3
Doña Carmen
  (Aguilar) 1 A2
Hostal Virgen del
  Rocío 15 C2
Jardín de la Muralla 10 E3
Montelirio 7 C2
Parador de Ronda 9 C1
San Francisco 13 B2
San Gabriel 14 D2

Restaurants

Bodega El Socorro 5 B1
La Leyenda 10 B2
Pedro Romero 3 B1
Tetería Al Zahra 9 B2
Tragabuches 8 C1
Tragatapas 4 C2

down by the Romero clan. While admission isn't cheap, if you have an interest in such things, it's well worth a visit. Apart from the thrill of walking out on to the arena itself, there's a museum with all sorts of memorabilia. You can also visit the stables, and, most interestingly, the bull pens, with their complex system of lifting gates operated from the safety of above.

Templete de la Virgen de los Dolores

Most of the other sights are across in the old town, but it's worth seeking out the Templete de la Virgen de los Dolores, also known as Los Ahorcados, on Calle Santa Cecilia. Built in the 18th century, it's a small chapel with a highly unusual façade. The Ionic columns are supported by strange birdmen and other figures, a product of late-Baroque mannerism influenced by Latin-American imagery.

Ciudad Vieja

Known simply as La Ciudad, the old part of Ronda is a tight knot of small streets and white houses, including several noble *palacios* and churches. A stretch of the city walls still encircles part of the area, beyond which extend green fields and the mountains of the sierra.

After crossing the bridge over the chasm, take a quick left and you'll soon come to the **Casa del Rey Moro** ① *Barrio de Padre Jesús s/n, T952-161002, daily 1000-1900, €4*. This evocatively faded mansion (also known as La Mina and Jardines de Forestier) with jutting wooden eaves was built in the 18th century over Moorish foundations. The principal attraction here is an impressive staircase hewn 80 m downwards through the rock to the river below. Some scholars say its function was merely so that slaves could fetch water for their Moorish master, but its real purpose is likely to have been as a sally-port in times of siege; legend attributes its construction to the king Abomelic. There are 232 steps down to the river, and they are slippery and steep. Once you're down you can admire the blue-green water from a tranquil small platform and look up at the town above. A fine landscaped garden is the other feature of the attraction.

On exiting the Casa del Rey Moro, you will enjoy the fine views of the town and countryside. Below is an old entrance gate into the city, which commemorates Felipe V. A short distance beyond, following the river away from town, are the 14th-century **Baños Arabes (Arab baths)** ① *Cuesta de Santo Domingo s/n, T656-950937, Mon-Fri 1000-1800 (1900 summer), Sat and Sun 1000-1500, €3*, preserving brick arches and star-shaped skylights.

Just above the Puerta de Felipe V is the **Palacio del Marqués de Salvatierra**, one of the more impressive of Ronda's many elegant buildings. Its 18th-century Baroque façade has been recently restored, and features four columns carved with caryatid-like figures, in this case apparently native American-inspired. Outside is a stone *crucero*.

Following this street along, you'll reach a small tower, the **Alminar de San Sebastián**, a former minaret of one of the town's many mosques. It's been capped by a later belfry but still preserves most of its original structure, including a horseshoe-arched window.

Near here, two grand and unusual buildings face each other across Plaza Duquesa de Parcent. The collegiate church of **Santa María la Mayor** ⓘ *Plaza Duquesa de Parcent s/n, T952-872246, daily 1000-1800 (2000 summer), closed Sun 1230-1400 €4*, was once Ronda's principal mosque. Converted into a church by Fernando, the Catholic Monarch, it retains little of its Moorish origins apart from an inscribed archway, the mihrab and the minaret, converted into a bell tower. Most striking is its double gallery looking out on to the square. The interior is mostly a blend of late Gothic and Renaissance arching; there's a fine elaborate choir, some poor frescoes, and an inlaid Churrigueresque *retablo*. Upstairs, behind the galleries, is an exhibition of polychrome sculpture.

On the same square are the long arcades of the **Ayuntamiento**, perhaps reminiscent of a row of shops for good reason, as it has been suggested that it was once a Moorish market.

Beyond here, the Ciudad comes to an end in the Barrio de San Francisco, which has a well-preserved section of walls and a fine sandstone-block church in **Iglesia del Espíritu Santo**. A gate leads out through the walls towards the countryside beyond. Back at Plaza Duquesa, head east to the **Museo Municipal** ⓘ *Plaza Mondragón s/n, T952-870818, Mon-Fri 1000-1800 (1900 summer), Sat and Sun 1000-1500, €3*, which is set in the Palacio de Mondragón, one of Ronda's most beautiful mansions. The building alone is worth the price of admission; it centres around two patios, the first with red arches and a well, the second with a wooden gallery and eaves, as well as colourful tilework. There's also a Moorish-style garden. The collection is a mixture of displays: the flora and fauna of the Sierra de los Nieves; a reconstruction of a late Bronze Age hut with thatched roof on stone foundations; of a cave; and a prehistoric metalworking furnace. One of the most important pieces is a seventh-century BC mould for making swords. There's also a resumé of Muslim funerary customs and a collection of Moorish gravestones.

There are several other museums in the Ciudad Vieja. The **Museo Lara** ⓘ *C Armiñán 29, T952-871263, www.museolara.org, daily 1100-2000 (1900 winter), €4*, could be described as a collection of collections, with a bizarre range of objects housed in yet another attractive *palacio*. There are swords, opera glasses, sewing machines, torture implements, witchcraft displays and typewriters among numerous other curios. There are flamenco shows here on spring and summer evenings. Nearby, the **Museo del Vino** ⓘ *C González Campos 2, T952 879 735, www.bodegaslasangrederonda.com, Mon-Thu 1030-1900, Fri 1100-1830, Sat 1030-1900, Sun 1100-1530, €5*, is a *bodega* with a pretty patio; the tour includes a tasting; the **Museo de Caza** is devoted to hunting, while the **Museo del Bandolero** pays homage to the famous bandits of the region. Lastly, the **Museo Joaquín Peinado** is a gallery with works by that *rondeño* painter of the Paris school.

Around Ronda → *For listings, see pages 76-79.*

The ruins of **Acinipo** ⓘ *Ctra MA-449 s/n, T951-041452, Wed-Sun 1000-1500, free*, also known as **Ronda la Vieja**, lie 12 km northwest of Ronda off the Sevilla road. An important Roman town in its day (the first century AD was its zenith), it later declined as Ronda's fortunes rose. Sprawled across a hilltop, most of the ruins are fragmentary, but what makes the visit worthwhile is the massive theatre with views across the sierra. There are also remains of earlier Iberian and Phoenician structures. There's almost no visitor information and opening hours are haphazard – check at the Ronda tourist office or by phone before setting out. Not much further is the strange and beautiful town of **Setenil de las Bodegas** in Cádiz province.

    Cueva de la Pileta ⓘ *Benaoján, T952-167343, daily 1000-1300, 1600-1700 (1800 summer), entry by guided tour on the hour in groups of up to 25, €7-8 depending on numbers, 1 hr*, an important cave 20 km southwest of Ronda, was discovered in 1905 by a local farmer. On following a stream of bats in the hope of collecting some of their dung as fertilizer, he came across a series of prehistoric paintings. The cave is 2 km long and further exploration has revealed a large quantity of art in various different chambers. While the limestone formations aren't the most spectacular you've ever seen, the visit is fascinating, and guided by a descendant of the original farmer. Commentary, in Spanish, and limited English, is intelligent and humorous. The oldest paintings date from the Palaeolithic – and range from 12,000 to 30,000 years old. You can see a horsehead, bulls, goats, a fish, and a seal. The oldest probably represents the earliest phase of Cro-Magnon presence in Europe. There are also Neolithic paintings – mostly geometric patterns and abstract forms, but also what appears to be a form of calendar. It's all the better for being able to peer at these paintings by lantern light before the inevitable interpretation centre is built. To get there, take a left off the A-574 (Sevilla) road not far below Ronda; it's signposted Benaoján. When you get to Benaoján, head through the village, then take a sharp left as you leave it on the other side. The cave is 5 km along this road; bat-phobes should stay in the car.

    As well as the excursions listed above, the white towns of Cádiz province, including Grazalema, are close at hand.

Ronda to Gaucín

One of the province's more spectacular drives heads from Ronda southwest towards Algeciras through a succession of whitewashed hilltop villages with a distinctly Moorish ambience. **Atajate**, some 18 km from Ronda, is typical, with a high 19th-century church and perspectives over olive groves, grapevines and chestnut woods. **Benadalid** boasts a castle that was strategically crucial in the Reconquista, while larger **Benalauría** and **Algatocín** have several fine buildings amid their narrow streets. A 13-km detour south from Algatocín, **Genalguacil** seems like another typical village from afar, until you arrive and find its streets, parks and plazas stocked full of sculptures of every type imaginable, a legacy of a biennial gathering of artists in the village. It's well worth the detour to see it. The most interesting of the towns, **Gaucín**, makes a tempting rural base and is dominated by its ruined fortress on a rocky crag high over town. From Gaucín, you can cross a valley via a spectacular road to the pretty town of Casares, near Estepona on the Costa del Sol, see page 51.

Ronda listings

For hotel and restaurant price codes and other relevant information, see pages 6-12.

⊖ Where to stay

Ronda *p70, map p72*

€€€€ Parador de Ronda, Plaza de España s/n, T952-877500, www.parador.es. Set in the former town hall on the very edge of the Tajo by the Puente Nuevo bridge, this *parador* has one of the most memorable locations of any Andalucían hotel. While its public areas still suffer from a municipal feel, the rooms are excellent, with comfortable furniture, polished floorboards, plenty of space and big beds. The pricier ones have balconies overlooking the gorge, and it's hard to beat the hotel pool, which is right on the lip of it.

€€€ Hotel Acinipo, C José Aparicio 7, T952-161002, www.hotelacinipo.com. This small modern hotel is right in the heart of the action, set in a quiet street between the bullring and Plaza de España. It's decorated with a contemporary but warm and colourful flair. The rooms have excellent facilities and are attractive with polished floorboards. Also boasts a fine restaurant, the **Atrium**.

€€€ Hotel Montelirio, C Tenorio 8, T952-873855, www.hotelmontelirio.com. Close to the bridge, and with rooms and spacious junior suites offering views (rooms without a view are not a great deal, so you might as well), this boutique hotel impresses on many levels, not least for its welcoming management. The more than decent restaurant has a terrace perched right on the edge of the ravine, and there's also a small pool. Recommended.

€€ Alavera de los Baños, C San Miguel s/n, T952-879143, www. alaveradelosbanos.com. Delightful small hotel with an organically minded restaurant, located between the town walls and the Baños Arabes. Rooms are charmingly and tastefully decorated and you'll get a warm welcome from the owners. Relaxing garden with a pool. Breakfast included. Recommended.

€€ Hotel Enfrente Arte, C Real 40, T952-879088, www.enfrentearte. com. This stylish and friendly hotel is painted throughout in bright pastel colours that define the funky mood of the place. The rooms are cheerful and comfortable and vary in size and price – some have views. There's a pool, pool table and internet access and, with a generous breakfast/brunch buffet and all beverages included, it's a delight. Recommended.

€€ Hotel Jardín de la Muralla, C Espíritu Santo 13, T952-872764, www.jardindelamuralla.com. A charming hotel set around a central patio, it has large, light rooms that are cheerfully furnished with curios and pictures. There's a lounge with a piano and a garden terrace. Breakfast is included. Good value.

€€ Hotel San Francisco, C María Cabrera 18, T952-873299, www. sanfranciscoronda.com. This well-run, central choice has a variety of rooms with colourful bedspreads and padded headboards. They are excellent value, have plenty of light and very good bathrooms, as well

as TV, heating and a/c. Rates include breakfast. Recommended for decent sleeping at a low price.

€€ Hotel San Gabriel, C Marqués de Moctezuma 19, T952-190392, www.hotelsangabriel.com. Beautifully restored and located townhouse run with real love by 3 siblings who grew up in it. A tastefully old-fashioned lounge has bookcases and old sofas. The rooms are elegant – the larger ones have colourful screens to make the space a bit more intimate. Bathrooms and facilities are top-grade without detracting from the old-world charm. Easy street parking nearby. Excellent continental breakfast (extra), and there's free internet access and Wi-Fi. Highly recommended.

€ Hostal Doña Carmen (Aguilar), C Naranja 28, T952-871994. Modernized *hostal* with good clean rooms and heating, run by a friendly family. There's another section with older, shabbier rooms (somewhat cheaper); these have shared bathroom and are fine value in summer but iceboxes in winter.

€ Hostal Virgen del Rocío, C Nueva 18, T952-877425, www. hostalvirgendelrocio.es. On a pedestrian street close to Plaza de España, this comfy *hostal* is decorated with *azulejos* and pot plants. The rooms are less adorned, with simple white beds, but have en suite, TV and telephone.

Camping
Camping El Sur, Ctra A369, Km 2, T952-875939, www.campingelsur. com. Open all the year, this excellent

campsite has a pool, bar, restaurant and tidy modern bungalows. It's 2 km out of town on the Algeciras road.

Ronda to Gaucín *p76*
€€ Hotel La Fructuosa, C Convento 67, Gaucín, T952-151072, www.la fructuosa.com. This excellent rural hotel is an appetizing place right in the heart of pretty Gaucín, 36 km southwest of Ronda, and a base for walking and driving exploration of the surrounding hills. All the rooms are different, offering great views and decorated with exquisite modern rural style. Facilities include free internet and Wi-Fi as well as a fabulous roof terrace; the included breakfast and the warm personal service also make this a standout. Recommended.

⏚ Restaurants

Ronda *p70, map p72*
Many of Ronda's restaurants are tourist traps. Avoid most of the ones along C Nueva.

€€€ Pedro Romero, C Virgen de la Paz 18, T952-871110, www. rpedroromero.com. The best of the restaurants along the main street near the bullring and predictably decorated with taurine memorabilia. Although it sees its fair share of tourists, it can't be faulted on quality. The bull's tail is particularly good, but anything with a local flavour is recommended. The lunchtime *menú* is €18, but the à la carte is more memorable.

€€€ Tragabuches, C José Aparicio 1, T952-190291, www.tragabuches.com. With an attractive modern dining area with big plate-glass windows looking out over the gardens by the bullring, this restaurant usually wins the foodies' vote as Ronda's most creative. The menu is a small one and changes often. The prices are high for Spain, but low for the quality on offer; try anything with local *setas* (wild mushrooms). What really gets gourmet hearts racing, however, is the *menú de degustación*. You'll get a meal to remember, with tapas followed by several courses, interspersed with palate-cleansers. Recommended.

€€ La Leyenda, C Los Remedios 7, T952-877894. An excellent Gaudí-inspired tapas bar, light and colourful with cut-glass lamps. The tapas are tasty and cheap; try the variety of smoked fish or whatever is the tapa of the day (€1). Recommended.

€€ Tragatapas, C Nueva 4, T952-878640. The delicious fare at this central tapas bar features plenty of innovation, with ox *tataki* taking its place alongside salmon with vanilla and lime or fried squid with broad beans. Recommended.

€ Bodega El Socorro, C Molina 4. Just off Plaza del Socorro, this warm and busy bar is decorated with farm tools. The tapas are excellent; try the spinach croquettes, prawn and bacon brochettes or the cold pasta salad.

Cafés
Tetería Al Zahra, C Las Tiendas 19. Open from 1600. An enticing Moorish-style teahouse with a large range of infusions, some sweet pastries and soothing music and decor.

ⓐ Entertainment

Ronda *p70, map p72*
Check the Culture section of the website www.turismoderonda.es for a list of upcoming events. The flamenco *peña* Tobalo organize weekly performances for about half the year; other more touristy spectacles running twice or thrice weekly from Mar to Oct are held in the **Museo Lara**.

ⓕ Festivals

Ronda *p70, map p72*
Early Sep Ronda's main fiesta, named in honour of **Pedro Romero** is celebrated with bullfights in 18th-century costumes. There's also a flamenco festival as part of it.

ⓦ What to do

Ronda *p70, map p72*
Bike hire
CycleRonda, C Serrato 3, T952-877814, www.cycleronda.com. Has a good variety of bikes for hire, including electric hybrids. Offers route information for the surrounding area.
Pangea, Pasaje Cayetano 10, T630-562705, www.pangeacentral.com. Offers outdoor activities in the surrounding area; check website for details.

Bullfighting
You'll need to be here in mid-May for the *feria* or in early Sep for the fiestas. Book tickets on www. riveraordonez.com (for the fiesta; box office opens 14 Aug or via brokers such as www.entradatoro.com).

ⓣ Transport

Ronda *p70, map p72*
Bus
There are 4 to 10 daily buses to **Málaga** (2 hrs), some direct. **Sevilla** is served 3-5 times daily (2 hrs 30 mins), and there are a couple of daily buses to **Marbella** and **Fuengirola**. Other destinations include **Grazalema** and **Ubrique** (2 a day, none on Sun), **Cádiz** via **Arcos de la Frontera** and **Jerez** 5 times daily, 1 to **Algeciras** via **Gaucín** and **Jimena de la Frontera**, and 6 to nearby **Setenil** (4 on Sat, none on Sun).

Train
Ronda is on the train line running from **Algeciras** to **Granada** via **Jimena de la Frontera** and **Antequera**. There are 3 daily trains to **Granada**, 2 hrs 30 mins, and 5 to **Algeciras**, 1 hr 45 mins, as well as connections to Bobadilla and then **Córdoba**, **Málaga**, **Madrid** and **Sevilla**.

Contents

Footprint features

Footnotes

Culture in Andalucía

Architecture

Spain's architectural heritage is one of Europe's richest and certainly its most diverse, due in large part to the dual influences of European Christian and Islamic styles during the eight centuries of Moorish presence in the peninsula. Another factor is economic: both during the *Reconquista* and in the wake of the discovery of the Americas, money seemed limitless and vast building projects were undertaken. Entire treasure fleets were spent in erecting lavish churches and monasteries on previously Muslim soil, while the relationships with Islamic civilization spawned some fascinating styles unique to Spain. The Moors adorned their towns with sensuous palaces, such as Granada's Alhambra, and elegant mosques, as well as employing compact climate-driven urban planning that still forms the hearts of most towns. In modern times Spain has shaken off the ponderous monumentalism of the Franco era and become something of a powerhouse of modern architecture.

Andalucía's finest early stone structures are in **Antequera** (see page 61), whose dolmens are extraordinarily monumental burial spaces built from vast slabs of stone. The dwellings of the period were less permanent structures of which little evidence remains, except at the remarkable site of Los Millares near Almería, a large Chalcolithic settlement, necropolis, and sophisticated associated fortifications that has provided valuable information about society in the third millennium BC. The first millennium BC saw the construction of further fortified settlements, usually on hilltops. Little remains of this period in Andalucía, as the towns were then occupied by the Romans and Moors.

Similarly, while the Phoenicians established many towns in southern Spain, their remains are few; they were so adept at spotting natural harbours that nearly all have been in continual use ever since, leaving only the odd foundations or breakwater. There are also few Carthaginian remains of note. Their principal base in Andalucía was Cádiz, but two millennia of subsequent occupation have taken their toll on the archaeological record.

The story of Spanish architecture really begins with the Romans, who colonized the peninsula and imposed their culture on it to a significant degree. More significant still is the legacy they left: architectural principles that endured and to some extent formed the basis for later peninsular styles.

There's not a wealth of outstanding monuments; Itálica, just outside Sevilla, and Baelo Claudia, on the Costa de la Luz, are impressive, if not especially well-preserved Roman towns. **Acinipo**, near Ronda (see page 75), has a large and spectacularly sited theatre, Carmona has a beautifully excavated necropolis, and Almuñécar has the ruins of its fish sauce factory on display. In many towns and villages you can see Roman fortifications and foundations under existing structures.

There are few architectural reminders of the Visigothic period, although it was far from a time of lawless barbarism. Germanic elements were added to Roman and local traditions and there was widespread building; the kings of the period commissioned many churches, but in Andalucía these were all demolished to make way for mosques.

The first distinct period of Moorish architecture in Spain is that of the Umayyads ruling as emirs, then as caliphs, from Córdoba from the eighth to 11th centuries. Although the Moors immediately set about building mosques, the earliest building still standing is Córdoba's Mezquita. Dating from the late ninth century, the ruined church at the mountain stronghold of **Bobastro** (see page 60) exhibits clear stylistic similarities with parts of the Mezquita and indicates that already a specifically *Andalusi* architecture was extant.

The period of the caliphate was the high point of Al-Andalus and some suitably sumptuous architecture remains. Having declared himself caliph, Abd al-Rahman III had the palace complex of Madinat az-Zahra built just outside of Córdoba. Now in ruins, excavation and reconstruction have revealed some of the one-time splendour, particularly of the throne room, which has arcades somewhat similar to those of the Mezquita and ornate relief designs depicting the Tree of Life and other vegetal motifs. The residential areas are centred around courtyards, a feature of Roman and Moorish domestic architecture that persists in Andalucía to this day.

The Mezquita had been added to by succeeding rulers, who enlarged it but didn't stray far from the original design. What is noticeable is a growing ornamentality, with use of multi-lobed arches, sometimes interlocking, and blind arcading on gateways. The mihrab was resituated and topped with a recessed dome, decorated with lavish mosaic work, possibly realized by Byzantine craftsmen. A less ornate mosque from this period can be seen in a beautiful hilltop setting at Almonaster la Real in the north of Huelva province.

Many defensive installations were also put up at this time: the castles of Tarifa and Baños de la Encina mostly date from this period. Bathhouses such as those of Jaén were also in use, although were modified in succeeding centuries. The typical Moorish *hammam* had a domed central space and vaulted chambers with star-shaped holes in the ceiling to admit natural light.

The *taifa* period, although politically chaotic, continued the rich architectural tradition of the caliphate. Málaga's **Alcazaba** (see page 22) preserved an 11th-century pavilion with delicate triple arches on slender columns. Elaborate stucco decoration, usually with repeating geometric or vegetal motifs, began to be used commonly during this time.

The Almoravids contributed little to Andalucían architecture, but the Almohads brought their own architectural modifications with them. Based in Sevilla, their styles were not as flamboyant and relied heavily on ornamental brickwork. The supreme example of the period is the Giralda tower that once belonged to the mosque in Sevilla and now forms part of the cathedral. The use of intricate wood-panelled ceilings began to be popular and the characteristic Andalucían *azulejo* decorative tiles were first used at this time. Over this period the horseshoe arch developed a point. The Almohads were great military architects and built or improved a large number of walls, fortresses and towers; these often have characteristic pointed battlements. The Torre del Oro in Sevilla is one of the most famous and attractive examples.

The climax of Moorish architecture ironically came when Al-Andalus was already doomed and had been reduced to the emirate of Granada. Under the Nasrid rulers of that city the sublime **Alhambra** was constructed (see page 64); a palace and pleasure garden that took elegance and sophistication in architecture to previously unseen levels. Nearly all the attention was focused on the interior of the buildings, which consisted of galleries and courtyards offset by water features and elegant gardens. The architectural high point of this and other buildings is the sheer intricacy of the stucco decoration in panels surrounding the windows and doorways. Another ennobling feature is *mocárabes*, a curious concave decoration of prisms placed in a cupola or ceiling and resembling natural crystal formations in caves. The Alcázar in Sevilla is also a good example of the period, though actually constructed in Christian Spain; it is very Nasrid in character and Granadan craftsmen certainly worked on it.

As the Christians gradually took back Andalucía, they introduced their own styles, developed in the north with substantial influence from France and Italy. The Romanesque barely features in Andalucía; it was the Gothic style that influenced post-Reconquista church building in the 13th, 14th and 15th centuries. It was combined with styles learned under the Moors to form an Andalucían fusion known as Gothic-*mudéjar*. Many of the region's churches are constructed on these lines, typically featuring a rectangular floor plan with a triple nave surrounded by pillars, a polygonal chancel and square chapels. Gothic exterior buttresses were used and many had a bell tower decorated with ornate brickwork reminiscent of the Giralda, which was also rebuilt during this period.

The Andalucían Gothic style differs from the rest of the peninsula in its basic principles. Whereas in the north, the 'more space, less stone, more light' philosophy pervaded, practical considerations demanded different solutions in the south. One of these was space; the cathedrals normally occupied the site of the former mosque, which had square ground plans and were hemmed in by other buildings. Another was defence – on the coast in particular, churches and cathedrals had to be ready to double as fortresses in case of attack, so sturdy walls were of more importance than stained glass. The redoubt of a cathedral at Almería is a typical example. Many of Andalucía's churches, built in the Gothic style, were heavily modified in succeeding centuries and present a blend of different architectures.

Mudéjar architecture spread quickly across Spain. Moorish architects and those who worked with them began to meld their Islamic tradition with the northern influences. The result is distinctive and pleasing, typified by the decorative use of brick and coloured tiles, with tall elegant bell towers a particular highlight. Another common feature is the highly elaborate wooden panelled ceilings, some of which are masterpieces. The word *artesonado* describes the most characteristic type of these. The style became popular nationwide; in certain areas, *mudéjar* remained a constant feature for over 500 years of building.

The final phase of Spanish Gothic was the Isabelline, or Flamboyant. Produced during and immediately after the reign of the Catholic Monarchs (hence the name), it borrowed decorative motifs from Islamic architecture to create an exuberant form characterized by highly elaborate façades carved with tendrils, sweeping curves and geometrical patterns. The Capilla Real in Granada is an example and the Palacio de Jabalquinto in Baeza is a superb demonstration of the style.

The 16th century was a high point in Spanish power and wealth, when it expanded across the Atlantic, tapping riches that must have seemed limitless. Spanish Renaissance architecture reflected this, leading from the late Gothic style into the elaborate peninsular style known as Plateresque. Although the style originally relied heavily on Italian models, it soon took on specifically Spanish features. The word refers particularly to the façades of civil and religious buildings, characterized by decoration of shields and other heraldic motifs, as well as geometric and naturalistic patterns such as shells. The term comes from the word for silversmith, *platero*, as the level of intricacy of the stonework approached that of jewellery. Arches went back to the rounded and columns and piers became a riot of foliage and 'grotesque' scenes.

A classical revival put an end to much of the elaboration, as Renaissance architects concentrated on purity. To classical Greek features such as fluted columns and pediments were added large Italianate cupolas and domes. Spanish architects were apprenticed to Italian masters and returned to Spain with their ideas. Elegant interior patios in *palacios* are an especially attractive feature of the style, to be found across the country. Andalucía is a particularly rich storehouse of this style, where the master Diego de Siloé designed numerous cathedrals and churches. The **palace of Carlos V** in the Alhambra grounds (see page 65) is often cited as one of the finest examples of Renaissance purity. One of Diego de Siloé's understudies, Andrés de Vandelvira, evolved into the über-architect of the Spanish Renaissance. The ensemble of palaces and churches he designed in Jaén province, particularly in the towns of Ubeda and Baeza, are unsurpassed in their sober beauty. Other fine 16th-century *palacios* can be found in nearly every town and city of Andalucía; often built in honey-coloured sandstone, these noble buildings were the homes of the aristocrats who had reaped the riches of the Reconquista and the new trade routes to the Americas.

The pure lines of this Renaissance classicism were soon to be transformed into a new style, Spanish Baroque. Although it started fairly soberly, it soon became rather ornamental, often being used to add elements to existing buildings. The Baroque was a time of great genius in architecture as in the other arts in Spain, as masters playfully explored the reaches of their imaginations; a strong reaction against the sober preceding style. Churches became ever larger, in part to justify the huge façades, and nobles indulged in one-upmanship, building ever-grander *palacios*. The façades themselves are typified by such features as pilasters (narrow piers descending to a point) and niches to hold statues. Andalucía has a particularly vast array of Baroque churches; Sevilla in particular bristles with them, while Cádiz cathedral is almost wholly built in this style. Smaller towns, such as Priego de Córdoba and Ecija, are also well endowed, as they both enjoyed significant agriculture-based prosperity during the period.

The Baroque became more ornate as time went on, reaching the extremes of Churrigueresque, named for the Churriguera brothers who worked in the late 17th and early 18th centuries. The result can be overelaborate but on occasion transcendentally beautiful. Vine tendrils and cherubs decorate façades and *retablos*, which seem intent on breaking every classical norm, twisting here, upside-down there and at their best seeming to capture motion.

Neoclassicism, encouraged by a new interest in the ancient civilizations of Greece and Rome, was an inevitable reaction to such *joie de vivre*. It again resorted to the cleaner lines of antiquity, which were used this time for public spaces as well as civic and religious buildings. Many plazas and town halls in Spain are in this style, which tended to flourish in the cities that were thriving in the late 18th and 19th centuries, such as Cádiz, whose elegant old town is largely in this style. The best examples use symmetry to achieve beauty and elegance, such as the Prado in Madrid, or Sevilla's tobacco factory, which bridges Baroque and neoclassical styles.

The late 19th century saw Catalan *modernista* architecture break the moulds in a startling way. At the forefront of the movement was Antoni Gaudí. Essentially a highly original interpretation of art nouveau, Gaudí's style featured naturalistic curves and contours enlivened with stylistic elements inspired by Muslim and Gothic architecture. There is little *modernista* influence in Andalucía, but more sober *fin de siècle* architecture can be seen in Almería, which was a prosperous industrial powerhouse at the time.

Awakened interest in the days of Al-Andalus led to the neo-Moorish (or neo-*mudéjar*) style being used for public buildings and private residences. The most evident example of this is the fine ensemble of buildings constructed in Sevilla for the 1929 Ibero-American exhibition. Budgets were thrown out the window and the lavish pavilions are sumptuously decorated. Similarly ornate is the theatre in Cádiz.

Elegance and whimsy never seemed to play much part in fascist architecture and during the Franco era Andalucía was subjected to an appalling series of ponderous concrete monoliths, all in the name of progress. A few avant-garde buildings managed to escape the drudgery from the 1950s on, but it was the dictator's death in 1975, followed by EEC membership in 1986, that really provided the impetus for change.

Andalucía is not at the forefront of Spain's modern architectural movements, but the World Expo in Sevilla in 1992 brought some of the big names in. Among the various innovative pavilions, Santiago Calatrava's sublime bridges stand out. The impressive Teatro de la Maestranza and public library also date from this period, while the newer Olympic stadium, and Málaga's **Picasso Museum** and **Centro de Arte Contemporáneo** (see pages 19 and 23) – both successful adaptations of older buildings – are more recent offerings. Sevilla's fantastic Parasol building, daringly built over a square in the old town, is the latest spectacular construction. Elsewhere, the focus has been on softening the harsh Francoist lines of the cities' 20th-century expansions. In most places this has been quietly successful. Much of the coast, however, is still plagued by the concrete curse, where planning laws haven't been strict enough in some places, and have been circumvented with a well-placed bribe in others.

Art

In the first millennium BC, Iberian cultures produced fine jewellery from gold and silver, as well as some remarkable sculpture and ceramics. These influences derived from contact with trading posts set up by the Phoenicians, who also left artistic evidence of their presence, mostly in the port cities they established. Similarly, the Romans brought their own artistic styles to the peninsula and there are many cultural remnants, including some fine sculpture and a number of elaborate mosaic floors. Later, the Visigoths were skilled artists and craftspeople and produced many fine pieces, most notably in metalwork.

The majority of the artistic heritage left by the Moors is tied up in their architecture (see above). As Islamic tradition has tended to veer away from the portrayal of human or animal figures, the norm was intricate applied decoration with calligraphic, geometric and vegetal themes predominating.

Superb panelled ceilings are a feature of Almohad architecture; a particularly attractive style being that known as *artesonado*, in which the concave panels are bordered with elaborate inlay work. During this period, glazed tiles known as *azulejos* began to be produced; these continue to be a feature of Andalucían craftsmanship.

The gradual process of the *Reconquista* brought Christian styles into Andalucía. Generally speaking, the Gothic, which had arrived in Spain both overland from France and across the Mediterranean from Italy, was the first post-Moorish style in Andalucía. Over time, Gothic sculpture achieved greater naturalism and became more ornate, culminating in the technical mastery of sculptors and painters, such as Pedro Millán, Pieter Dancart (who is responsible for the massive altarpiece of Sevilla's cathedral) and Alejo Fernández, all of whom were from or heavily influenced by northern Europe.

Though to begin with, the finest artists were working in Northern Spain, Andalucía soon could boast several notable figures of its own. In the wake of the Christian conquest of Granada, the Catholic Monarchs and their successor Carlos V went on a building spree. The Spanish Renaissance drew heavily on the Italian but developed its own style. Perhaps the finest 16th-century figure is Pedro de Campaña, a Fleming whose exalted talent went largely unrecognized in his own time. His altarpiece of the Purification of Mary in Sevilla's cathedral is particularly outstanding. The Italian sculptor Domenico Fancelli was entrusted by Carlos to carve the tombs of Fernando and Isabel in Granada; these are screened by a fine *reja* (grille) by Maestro Bartolomé, a Jaén-born artist who has several such pieces in Andalucían churches. The best-known 16th-century Spanish artist, the Cretan Domenikos Theotokopoulos (El Greco), has a few works in Andalucía, but the majority are in Toledo and Madrid.

As the Renaissance progressed, naturalism in painting increased, leading into the Golden Age of Spanish art. As Sevilla prospered on New World riches, the city became a centre for artists, who found wealthy patrons in abundance. Pre-eminent among all was Diego Rodríguez de Silva Velásquez (1599-1660), who started his career there before moving to Madrid to become a court painter. Another remarkable painter working in Sevilla was Francisco de Zurbarán (1598-1664) whose idiosyncratic style often focuses on superbly rendered white garments in a dark, brooding background, a metaphor for the subjects themselves, who were frequently priests. During Zurbarán's later years, he was eclipsed in the Sevilla popularity stakes by Bartolomé Esteban Murillo (1618-1682). While at first glance his paintings can seem heavy on the sentimentality, they tend to focus on the space between the central characters, who interact with glances or gestures of great power and meaning. Juan Valdés Leal painted many churches and monasteries in Sevilla; his greatest works are the macabre realist paintings in the Hospital de la Caridad. The sombre tone struck by these works reflects the decline of the once-great mercantile city.

At this time, the sculptor Juan Martínez Montañés carved numerous figures, *retablos* and *pasos* (ornamental floats for religious processions) in wood. Pedro Roldán, Juan de Mesa and Pedro de Mena were other important Baroque sculptors from this period, as was Alonso Cano, a crotchety but talented painter and sculptor working from Granada. The main focus of this medium continued to be ecclesiastic; *retablos* became ever larger and more ornate, commissioned by nobles to gain favour with the church and improve their chances in the afterlife.

The 18th and early 19th centuries saw fairly characterless art produced under the new dynasty of Bourbon kings. Tapestry production increased markedly but never scaled the heights of the earlier Flemish masterpieces. One man who produced pictures for tapestries was the master of 19th-century art, Francisco Goya. Goya was a remarkable figure whose finest works included both paintings and etchings; there's a handful of his work scattered around Andalucía's galleries, but the best examples are in Madrid's Prado and in the north.

After Goya, the 19th century produced few works of note as Spain tore itself apart in a series of brutal wars and conflicts. Perhaps in reaction to this, the *costumbrista* tradition developed; these painters and writers focused on portraying Spanish life; their depictions often revolving around nostalgia and stereotypes. Among the best were the Bécquer family: José; his cousin Joaquín; and his son Valeriano, whose brother Gustavo Adolfo was one of the period's best-known poets.

The early 20th century saw the rise of Spanish modernism and surrealism, much of it driven from Catalunya. While architects such as Gaudí managed to combine their discipline with art, it was one man from Málaga who had such an influence on 20th-century painting that he is arguably the most famous artist in the world. Pablo Ruiz Picasso (1881-1973) is notable not just for his artistic genius, but also for his evolution through different styles. Training in Barcelona, but doing much of his work in Paris, his initial Blue Period was fairly sober and subdued, named for predominant use of that colour. His best early work, however, came in his succeeding Pink Period, where he used brighter tones to depict the French capital. He moved on from this to become a pioneer of cubism. Drawing on non-western forms, cubism forsook realism for a new form of three-dimensionality, trying to show subjects from as many different angles as possible. Picasso then moved on to more surrealist forms. He continued painting right throughout his lifetime and produced an incredible number of works. One of his best-known paintings is *Guernica*, a nightmarish ensemble of terror-struck animals and people that he produced in abhorrence at the Nationalist bombing of the defenceless Basque town in April 1937. The **Picasso Museum** in Málaga (see page 19) displays a range of his works.

A completely different contemporary was the Córdoban Julio Romero de Torres, a painter who specialized in sensuous depictions of Andalucían women, usually fairly unencumbered by clothing. A more sober 20th-century painter was Daniel Vásquez Díaz, a Huelvan who adorned the walls of La Rábida monastery with murals on the life of Columbus.

The Civil War was to have a serious effect on art in Spain, as a majority of artists sided with the Republic and fled Spain with their defeat. Franco was far from an enlightened patron of the arts and his occupancy was a monotonous time. Times have changed, however, and the regional governments, including the Andalucían, are extremely supportive of local artists these days and the museums in each provincial capital usually have a good collection of modern works.

Literature

The peninsula's earliest known writers lived under the Roman occupation. Of these, two of the best known hailed from Córdoba: Seneca the Younger (3 BC-AD 65), the Stoic poet, philosopher and statesman who lived most of his life in Rome, and his nephew Lucan (AD 39-AD 65), who is known for his verse history of the wars between Caesar and Pompey, *Bellum Civile*. Both were forced to commit suicide for plotting against the emperor Nero. After the fall of Rome, one of the most remarkable of all Spain's literary figures was the bishop of Sevilla, San Isidoro, whose works were classic texts for over a millennium.

In Al-Andalus a flourishing literary culture existed under the Córdoba caliphate and later. Many important works were produced by Muslim and Jewish authors; some were to have a large influence on European knowledge and thought. The writings of Ibn Rushd (Averroes; 1126-1198) were of fundamental importance, asserting that the study of philosophy was not incompatible with religion and commentating extensively on Aristotle. The discovery of his works a couple of centuries on by Christian scholars led to the rediscovery of Aristotle and played a triggering role in the Renaissance. His contemporary in Córdoba, Maimonides (1135-1204) was one of the foremost Jewish writers of all time; writing on Jewish law, religion and spirituality in general and medicine, he remains an immense and much-studied figure. Another important Jewish writer was the philosopher and poet Judah ha-Levi (1075-1141); although born in the north, he spent much of his time writing in Granada and Córdoba. Throughout the Moorish period, there were many chronicles, treatises and studies written by Arab authors, but poetry was the favoured form of literary expression. Well-crafted verses, often about love and frequently quite explicit, were penned by such authors as the Sevilla king Al-Mu'tamid and the Córdoban Ibn Hazm.

After the Moors, however, Andalucía didn't really produce any literature of note until the so-called Golden Age of Spanish writing, which came in the wake of the discovery of the Americas and the flourishing of trade and wealth;

Antonio Machado

*Mi infancia son recuerdos de un patio
de Sevilla, / y un huerto claro donde
madura el limonero; / mi juventud,
veinte años en tierras de Castilla; / mi
historia, algunos casos que recordar
no quiero*

*My childhood is memories of a patio
in Sevilla, / and of a light-filled garden
where the lemon tree grows / My
youth, twenty years in the lands of
Castilla / My story, some happenings I
wish not to remember*

Along with Federico García Lorca,
Antonio Machado was Spain's
greatest 20th-century poet. Part of
the so-called Generation of '98 who
struggled to re-evaluate Spain in
the wake of losing its last colonial
possessions in 1898, he was born in
1875 in Sevilla.

After moving to France, Machado
returned to live in Soria, in Castilla;
much of his poetry is redolent of the
harsh landscapes of that region. His
solitude was exacerbated when his
young wife Leonor died after three
years of marriage. He then moved to
Baeza, where he taught French in a
local school. Like the poetry written
in Soria, his work in Andalucía
reflected his profound feelings for
the landscape.

Machado was a staunch defender
of the Republic and became
something of a bard of the Civil War.
Forced to flee with thousands of
refugees as the Republic fell, he died
not long after, in 1939, in a *pensión* in
southern France. His will to live was
dealt a bitter blow by the triumph of
fascism, while his health had suffered
badly during the trying journey.

patronage was crucial for writers in those days. The most notable poet of the
period is the Córdoban Luis de Góngora (1561-1627), whose exaggerated,
affected style is deeply symbolic (and sometimes almost inaccessible). His
work has been widely appreciated recently and critics tend to label him the
greatest of all Spanish poets, though he still turns quite a few people off.

The extraordinary life of Miguel de Cervantes (1547-1616) marks the start of
a rich period of Spanish literature. *Don Quijote* came out in serial form in 1606
and is rightly considered one of the finest novels ever written; it's certainly the
widest-read Spanish work. Cervantes spent plenty of time in Andalucía and
some of his *Novelas Ejemplares* are short stories set in Sevilla.

The Sevillian, Lope de Rueda (1505-1565), was in many ways Spain's first
playwright. He wrote comedies and paved the way for the explosion of Spanish
drama under the big three – Lope de Vega, Tirso de la Molina and Calderón de
la Barca – when public theatres opened in the early 17th century.

The 18th century was not such a rich period for Andalucían or Spanish writing
but in the 19th century the *costumbrista* movement (see page 89) produced

several fine works, among them *La Gaviota* (the Seagull), by Fernán Caballero, who was actually a Sevilla-raised woman named Cecilia Böhl von Faber, and *Escenas Andaluzas* (Andalucían Scenes), by Serafín Estébanez Calderón. Gustavo Adolfo Bécquer died young having published just one volume of poetry, popular, yearning works about love. Pedro Antonio de Alarcón (1833-1901), who hailed from Guadix, is most famous for his work *The Three-Cornered Hat*, a light and amusing tale which draws heavily on Andalucían customs and characters; it was also made into a popular ballet.

At the end of the 19th century, Spain lost the last of its colonial possessions after revolts and a war with the USA. This event, known as the Disaster, had a profound impact on the nation, and its date, 1898, gave its name to a generation of writers and artists. This group sought to express what Spain was and had been and to achieve new perspectives for the 20th century. One of their number was Antonio Machado (1875-1939), one of Spain's greatest poets; see box, page 91.

Another excellent poet of this time was Juan Ramón Jiménez (1881-1958), from Moguer in Huelva province, who won the Nobel Prize in 1956. His finest work is the long prose poem *Platero y Yo*, a lyrical portrait of the town and the region conducted as a conversation between the writer and his donkey. He was forced into exile by the Spanish Civil War.

The Granadan Federico García Lorca was a young poet and playwright of great ability and lyricism with a gypsy streak in his soul. His play *Bodas de Sangre* (Blood Wedding) sits among the finest Spanish drama ever written and his verse ranges from the joyous to the haunted and draws heavily on Andalucían folk traditions. Lorca was shot by fascist thugs in Granada just after the outbreak of hostilities in the Civil War: one of the most poignant of the thousands of atrocities committed in that bloody conflict.

Lorca was associated with the so-called Generation of 27, another loose grouping of artists and writers. One of their number was Rafael Alberti (1902-1999), a poet from El Puerto de Santa María and a close friend of Lorca's. Achieving recognition with his first book of poems, *Mar y Tierra*, Alberti was a Communist (who once met Stalin) and fought on the Republican side in the Civil War. He was forced into exile at the end of the war, only returning to Spain in 1978. Other Andalucían poets associated with this movement were the neo-romantic Luis Cernuda (1902-1963) and Vicente Aleixandre (1898-1984), winner of the 1977 Nobel Prize for his surrealist-influenced free verse. Both men were from Sevilla.

Although Aleixandre stayed in Spain, despite his poems being banned for a decade, the exodus and murder of the country's most talented writers was a heavy blow for literature. The greatest novelists of the Franco period, Camilo José Cela and Miguel Delibes, both hailed from the north, but in more recent times Andalucía has come to the fore again with Antonio Múñoz Molina (born

1956) from Ubeda in Jaén province. His *Ardor Guerrero* (*Warrior Lust*) is a bitter look at military service, while his highly acclaimed *Sepharad* is a collection of interwoven stories broadly about the Diaspora and Jewish Spain and set in various locations ranging from concentration camps to rural Andalucían villages.

Music and dance

Flamenco

Few things symbolize the mysteries of Andalucía like flamenco but, as with the region itself, much has been written that is over-romanticized, patronizing or just plain untrue. Like bullfighting, flamenco as we know it is a fairly young art, having basically developed in the 19th century. It is constantly evolving and there have been significant changes in its performance in the last century, which makes the search for classic flamenco a bit of a wild goose chase. Rather, the element to search for is authentic emotion and, beyond this, *duende*, an undefinable passion that carries singer and watchers away in a whirlwind of raw feeling, with a devil-may-care sneer at destiny.

Though there have been many excellent *payo* flamenco artists, its history is primarily a gypsy one. It was developed among the gypsy population in the Sevilla and Cádiz area but clearly includes elements of cultures encountered further away.

Flamenco consists of three basic components: *el cante* (the song), *el toque* (the guitar) and *el baile* (the dance). In addition, *el jaleo* provides percussion sounds through shouts, clicking fingers, clapping and footwork (and, less traditionally, castanets). Flamenco can be divided into four basic types: *tonás*, *siguiriyas*, *soleá* and *tangos*, which are characterized by their *comps* or form, rhythm and accentuation and are either *cante jondo* (emotionally deep)/*cante grande* (big) or *cante ligero* (lighter)/*cante chico* (small). Related to flamenco, but not in a pure form, are *sevillanas*, danced till you drop at Feria, and *rocieras*, which are sung on (and about) the annual *romería* pilgrimage to El Rocío.

For a foreigner, perhaps the classic image of flamenco is a woman in a theatrical dress clicking castanets. A more authentic image is of a singer and guitarist, both sitting rather disconsolately on ramshackle chairs, or perhaps on a wooden box to tap out a rhythm. The singer and the guitarist work together, sensing the mood of the other and improvising. A beat is provided by clapping of hands or tapping of feet. If there's a dancer, he or she will lock into the mood of the others and vice versa. The dancing is stop-start, frenetic: the flamenco can reach crescendoes of frightening intensity when it seems the singer will have a stroke, the dancer is about to commit murder, and the guitarist may never find it back to the world of the sane. These outbursts of passion are seen to their fullest in *cante jondo*, the deepest and saddest form of flamenco.

After going through a moribund period during the mid-20th century, flamenco was revived by such artists as Paco de Lucía, and the gaunt, heroin-addicted genius Camarón de la Isla, while the flamenco theatre of Joaquín Cortés put purists' noses firmly out of joint but achieved worldwide popularity. More recently, Diego 'El Cigala' carries on Camarón's angst-ridden tradition. Fusions of flamenco with other styles have been a feature of recent years, with the flamenco-rock of Ketama and the flamenco-chillout of Málaga-based Chambao achieving notable success. Granada's late Enrique Morente, a flamenco artist from the old school, outraged purists with his willingness to experiment with other artists and musical forms; his release 'Omega' brought in a punk band to accompany him and featured flamenco covers of Leonard Cohen hits.

Other music
Music formed a large part of cultural life in the days of the Córdoba emirate and caliphate. The earliest known depiction of a lute comes from an ivory bottle dated around AD 968; the musician Ziryab, living in the 11th century, made many important modifications to the lute, including the addition of a fifth double-string.

Like other art forms, music enjoyed something of a golden age under the early Habsburg monarchs. It was during this period that the five-string Spanish guitar came to be developed and the emergence of a separate repertoire for this instrument.

In 1629 Lope de Vega wrote the libretto for the first Spanish opera, which was to become a popular form. A particular Spanish innovation was the *zarzuela*, a musical play with speech and dancing. It became widely popular in the 19th century and is still performed in the larger cities. Spain's contribution to opera has been very important and continues to this day, producing a number of world-class singers such as Montserrat Caballé, Plácido Domingo, José Carreras and Teresa Berganza.

The Cádiz-born Manuel de Falla is the greatest figure in the history of a country that has produced few classical composers. He drew heavily on Andalucían themes and culture and also helped keep flamenco traditions alive.

De Falla's friendship with Debussy in Paris led to the latter's work *Ibéria*, which, although the Frenchman never visited Spain, was described by Lorca as very evocative of Andalucía. It was the latest of many Andalucía-inspired compositions, which include Bizet's *Carmen*, from the story by Prosper Merimée, and Rossini's *The Barber of Seville*, based on the play by Beaumarchais.

Contemporary music
Flamenco aside, Andalucía doesn't have a cutting-edge contemporary music scene. Most bars and *discotecas* play a repetitive selection of Spanish and

Latin-American pop, much of it derived from a series of phenomenally popular talent-quest TV shows.

In contrast, the Andalucían Joaquín Sabina is a heavyweight singer-songwriter who works both solo and in collaboration with other musicians. His songs draw on Andalucían folk traditions and he is deeply critical of modern popular culture. His gravelly voice is distinctive and has deservedly won him worldwide fame.

Basic Spanish for travellers

Learning Spanish is a useful part of the preparation for a trip to Spain and no volumes of dictionaries, phrase books or word lists will provide the same enjoyment as being able to communicate directly with the people of the country you are visiting. It is a good idea to make an effort to grasp the basics before you go. As you travel you will pick up more of the language and the more you know, the more you will benefit from your stay.

Vowels

a	as in English cat
e	as in English best
i	as the ee in English feet
o	as in English shop
u	as the oo in English food
ai	as the i in English ride
ei	as ey in English they
oi	as oy in English toy

Consonants

Most consonants can be pronounced more or less as they are in English. The exceptions are:

g	before e or i is the same as j
h	is always silent (except in ch as in chair)
j	as the ch in Scottish loch
ll	as the y in yellow
ñ	as the ni in English onion
rr	trilled much more than in English
x	depending on its location, pronounced x, s, sh or j

Spanish words and phrases

Greetings, courtesies

hello	*hola*	thank you (very much)	*(muchas) gracias*
good morning	*buenos días*		
good afternoon/ evening	*buenas tardes/ noches*	I speak a little Spanish	*hablo un poco de español*
goodbye	*adiós/ hasta luego*	I don't speak Spanish	*no hablo español*
pleased to meet you	*encantado/a*	do you speak English?	*¿hablas inglés?*
how are you?	*¿cómo estás?*	I don't understand	*no entiendo*
I'm called ...	*me llamo ...*	please speak slowly	*habla despacio por favor*
what is your name?	*¿cómo te llamas?*		
I'm fine, thanks	*muy bien, gracias*	I am very sorry	*lo siento mucho/ discúlpame*
yes/no	*sí/no*		
please	*por favor*	what do you want?	*¿qué quieres?*

I want/would like	*quiero/quería*	good/bad	*bueno/malo*
I don't want it	*no lo quiero*		

Basic questions and requests

have you got a room for two people?
¿tienes una habitación para dos personas?

how do I get to_?
¿cómo llego a_?

how much does it cost?
¿cuánto cuesta? ¿cuánto es?

is VAT included?
¿el IVA está incluido?

when does the bus leave (arrive)?
¿a qué hora sale (llega) el autobús?

when? *¿cuándo?*

where is_? *¿dónde está_?*

where can I buy?
¿dónde puedo comprar...?

where is the nearest petrol station?
¿dónde está la gasolinera más cercana?

why? *¿por qué?*

Basic words and phrases

bank	*el banco*	note/coin	*el billete/ la moneda*
bathroom/toilet	*el baño*	police (policeman)	*la policía (el policía)*
to be	*ser, estar*		
bill	*la factura/ la cuenta*	post office	*el correo*
cash	*efectivo*	public telephone	*el teléfono público*
cheap	*barato/a*		
credit card	*la tarjeta de crédito*	shop	*la tienda*
		supermarket	*el supermercado*
exchange rate	*el tipo de cambio*	there is/are	*hay*
		there isn't/aren't	*no hay*
expensive	*caro/a*	ticket office	*la taquilla*
to go	*ir*	traveller's cheques	*los cheques de viaje*
to have	*tener, haber*		
market	*el mercado*		

Getting around

aeroplane	*el avión*	bus	*el bus/ el autobús/ el camión*
airport	*el aeropuerto*		
arrival/departure	*la llegada/ salida*		
avenue	*la avenida*	corner	*la esquina*
border	*la frontera*	customs	*la aduana*
bus station	*la estación de autobuses*	left/right	*izquierda/ derecha*
		ticket	*el billete*

empty/full	vacío/lleno	to park	aparcar
highway, main road	la carretera	passport	el pasaporte
insurance	el seguro	petrol/gasoline	la gasolina
insured person	el asegurado/ la asegurada	puncture	el pinchazo
		street	la calle
luggage	el equipaje	that way	por allí
motorway, freeway	el autopista/ autovía	this way	por aquí
		tyre	el neumático
north/south/ west/east	el norte, el sur, el oeste, el este	unleaded	sin plomo
		waiting room	la sala de espera
oil	el aceite	to walk	caminar/andar

Accommodation

air conditioning	el aire acondicionado	room/bedroom	la habitación
		sheets	las sábanas
all-inclusive	todo incluido	shower	la ducha
bathroom, private	el baño privado	soap	el jabón
bed, double	la cama matrimonial	toilet	el inódoro
		toilet paper	el papel higiénico
blankets	las mantas		
to clean	limpiar	towels, clean/dirty	las toallas limpias/ sucias
dining room	el comedor		
hotel	el hotel		
noisy	ruidoso	water, hot/cold	el agua caliente/fría
pillows	las almohadas		
restaurant	el restaurante		

Health

aspirin	la aspirina	diarrhoea	la diarrea
blood	la sangre	doctor	el médico
chemist	la farmacia	fever/sweat	la fiebre/ el sudor
condoms	los preservativos, los condones		
		pain	el dolor
contact lenses	los lentes de contacto	head	la cabeza
		period	la regla
contraceptives	los anticonceptivos	sanitary towels	las toallas femininas
contraceptive pill	la píldora anticonceptiva	stomach	el estómago

Family

family	*la familia*	boyfriend/girlfriend	*el novio/*
brother/sister	*el hermano/*		*la novia*
	la hermana	friend	*el amigo/*
daughter/son	*la hija/el hijo*		*la amiga*
father/mother	*el padre/*	married	*casado/a*
	la madre	single/unmarried	*soltero/a*
husband/wife	*el esposo*		
	(marido)/		
	la mujer		

Months, days and time

January	*enero*	July	*julio*
February	*febrero*	August	*agosto*
March	*marzo*	September	*septiembre*
April	*abril*	October	*octubre*
May	*mayo*	November	*noviembre*
June	*junio*	December	*diciembre*

Monday	*lunes*	at one o'clock	*a la una*
Tuesday	*martes*	at half past two	*a las dos y*
Wednesday	*miércoles*		*media*
Thursday	*jueves*	at a quarter to three	*a las tres*
Friday	*viernes*		*menos cuarto*
Saturday	*sábado*	it's one o'clock	*es la una*
Sunday	*domingo*	it's seven o'clock	*son las siete*
		it's six twenty	*son las seis y*
			veinte
		it's five to nine	*son las nueve*
			menos cinco
		in ten minutes	*en diez minutos*
		five hours	*cinco horas*
		does it take long?	*¿tarda mucho?*

Numbers

one	*uno*	sixteen	*dieciséis*
two	*dos*	seventeen	*diecisiete*
three	*tres*	eighteen	*dieciocho*
four	*cuatro*	nineteen	*diecinueve*
five	*cinco*	twenty	*veinte*
six	*seis*	twenty-one	*veintiuno*
seven	*siete*	thirty	*treinta*
eight	*ocho*	forty	*cuarenta*
nine	*nueve*	fifty	*cincuenta*
ten	*diez*	sixty	*sesenta*
eleven	*once*	seventy	*setenta*
twelve	*doce*	eighty	*ochenta*
thirteen	*trece*	ninety	*noventa*
fourteen	*catorce*	hundred	*cien/ciento*
fifteen	*quince*	thousand	*mil*

Food glossary

A

acedía   small wedge sole

aceite   oil; *aceite de oliva* is olive oil and *aceite de girasol* is sunflower oil

aceitunas   olives, also sometimes called *olivas*. The best kind are unripe green *manzanilla*, particularly when stuffed with anchovy, *rellenas con anchoas*

adobo   marinated fried nuggets usually dogfish (*cazón*); delicious

agua   water

aguacate   avocado

ahumado   smoked; *tabla de ahumados* is a mixed plate of smoked fish

ajillo (al)   cooked in garlic, most commonly *gambas* or *pollo*

ajo   garlic, *ajetes* are young garlic shoots, often in a *revuelto*

ajo arriero   a simple sauce of garlic, paprika and parsley

ajo blanco   a chilled garlic and almond soup, a speciality of Málaga

albóndigas   meatballs

alcachofa/ alcaucil   artichoke

alcaparras   capers

aliño   any salad marinated in vinegar, olive oil and salt; often made with egg or potato, with chopped onion, peppers and tomato

alioli   a tasty sauce made from raw garlic blended with oil and egg yolk; also called *ajoaceite*

almejas   name applied to various species of small clams, often cooked with garlic, parsley and white wine

almendra   almond

alubias   broad beans

anchoa   preserved anchovy

añejo   aged (of cheeses, rums, etc)

angulas   baby eels, a delicacy that has become scarce and expensive. Far more common are *gulas*, false *angulas* made from putting processed fish through a spaghetti machine; squid ink is used for authentic colouring

anís   aniseed, commonly used to flavour biscuits and liqueurs

arroz   rice; *arroz con leche* is a sweet rice pudding

asado   roast. An *asador* is a restaurant specializing in charcoal-roasted meat and fish

atún   blue-fin tuna

azúcar   sugar

B

bacalao   salted cod, either superb or leathery

berberechos   cockles

berenjena   aubergine/eggplant

besugo   red bream

bistec   steak. *Poco hecho* is rare, *al punto* is medium rare, *regular* is medium, *muy hecho* is well done

bizcocho   sponge cake or biscuit

bocadillo/ bocata   a crusty filled roll

bogavante   lobster

bonito   atlantic bonito, a small tuna fish

boquerones   fresh anchovies, often served filleted in garlic and oil

botella	bottle	**chipirones**	small squid, often served *en su tinta*, in its own ink, mixed with butter and garlic
(a la) brasa	cooked on a griddle over coals, sometimes you do it yourself	**chocolate**	a popular afternoon drink; also slang for hashish
buey	ox	**choco**	cuttlefish

C

caballa	mackerel	**chorizo**	a red sausage, versatile and of varying spiciness (*picante*)
cacahuetes	peanuts	**choto**	roast kid
café	coffee; *solo* is black, served espresso-style; *cortado* adds a dash of milk, *con leche* more; *americano* is a long black coffee	**chuleta/ chuletilla**	chop
		chuletón	a massive T-bone steak, often sold by weight
calamares	squid	**churrasco**	barbecued meat, often ribs with a spicy sauce
caldereta	a stew of meat or fish usually made with sherry; *venao* (venison) is commonly used, and delicious	**churro**	a fried dough-stick usually eaten with hot chocolate (*chocolate con churros*). Usually eaten as a late afternoon snack (*merienda*), but sometimes for breakfast
caldo	a thin soup		
callos	tripe		
caña	a glass of draught beer	**cigala**	giant prawn
cangrejo	crab; occasionally river crayfish	**ciruela**	plum
		cochinillo	suckling pig
caracol	snail; very popular in Sevilla *cabrillas*, *burgaos*, and *blanquillos* are popular varieties	**cocido**	a heavy stew, usually of meat and chickpeas/beans; *sopa de cocido* is the broth
		codorniz	quail
caramelos	boiled sweets	**cogollo**	lettuce heart
carne	meat	**comida**	lunch
carta	menu	**conejo**	rabbit
casero	home-made	**congrio**	conger eel
castañas	chestnuts	**cordero**	lamb
cava	sparkling wine, mostly produced in Catalunya	**costillas**	ribs
		crema catalana	a lemony crème brûlée
cazuela	a stew, often of fish or seafood	**criadillas**	hog or bull testicles
cebolla	onion	**croquetas**	deep-fried crumbed balls of meat, béchamel, seafood, or vegetables
cena	dinner		
centollo	spider crab	**cuchara**	spoon
cerdo	pork	**cuchillo**	knife
cerezas	cherries	**cuenta** (la)	the bill
cerveza	beer		
champiñón	mushroom		

D

desayuno	breakfast
dorada	a species of bream (gilthead)
dulce	sweet

E

ecológico	organic
embutido	any salami-type sausage
empanada	a pie, pasty-like (*empanadilla*) or in large flat tins and sold by the slice; *atun* or *bonito* is a common filling, as is ham, mince or seafood
ensalada	salad; *mixta* is usually a large serve of a bit of everything; excellent option
ensaladilla rusa	Russian salad, with potato, peas and carrots in mayonnaise
escabeche	pickled in wine and vinegar
espárragos	asparagus, white and usually canned
espinacas	spinach
estofado	braised, often in stew form

F

fabada	the most famous of Asturian dishes, a hearty stew of beans, *chorizo*, and *morcilla*
fideuá	a bit like a paella but with noodles
filete	steak
fino	the classic dry sherry
flamenquín	a fried and crumbed finger of meat stuffed with ham
flan	the ubiquitous crème caramel, great when home-made (*casero*), awful when it's not
foie	fattened goose liver; often made into a thick gravy sauce
frambuesas	raspberries
fresas	strawberries
frito/a	fried
fruta	fruit

G

galletas	biscuits
gallo	rooster, also the flatfish megrim
gambas	prawns
garbanzos	chickpeas, often served in *espinacas con garbanzos*, a spicy spinach dish that is a signature of Seville
gazpacho	a cold garlicky tomato soup, very refreshing
granizado	popular summer drink, like a frappé fruit milkshake
guisado/ guiso	stewed/a stew
guisantes	peas

H

habas	broad beans, often deliciously stewed *con jamón*, with ham
harina	flour
helado	ice cream
hígado	liver
higo	fig
hojaldre	puff pastry
horno (al)	oven (baked)
hueva	fish roe
huevo	egg

I/J

ibérico	see *jamón*; the term can also refer to other pork products
infusión	herbal tea
jabalí	wild boar
jamón	ham; *jamón York* is cooked British-style ham. Far better is cured *jamón serrano*; top-grade *ibérico* ham comes from Iberian pigs in western Spain fed on acorns *bellotas*)
judías verdes	green beans
Jerez (al)	cooked in sherry

L

langosta	crayfish
langostinos	king prawns
lechazo	milk-fed lamb
leche	milk
lechuga	lettuce
lengua	tongue
lenguado	sole
lentejas	lentils
limón	lemon
lomo	loin, usually sliced pork, sometimes tuna
lubina	sea bass

M

macedonia de frutas	fruit salad, usually tinned
manchego	Spain's national cheese; hard, whitish and made from ewe's milk
manitas (de cerdo)	pork trotters
mantequilla	butter
manzana	apple
manzanilla	the dry, salty sherry from Sanlúcar de Barrameda; also, confusingly, camomile tea and the tastiest type of olive
marisco	shellfish
mejillones	mussels
melocotón	peach, usually canned and served in *almíbar* (syrup)
melva	frigate mackerel, often served tinned or semi-dried
menestra	a vegetable stew, usually served like a minestrone without the liquid; vegetarians will be annoyed to find that it's often seeded with ham and bits of pork
menú	a set meal, usually consisting of 3 or more courses, bread and wine or water
menudo	tripe stew, usually with chickpeas and mint

merluza	hake is to Spain as rice is to southeast Asia
mero	grouper
miel	honey
migas	breadcrumbs, fried and often mixed with lard and meat to form a delicious rural dish of the same name
Mojama	salt-cured tuna, most common in Cádiz province
mollejas	sweetbreads; ie the pancreas of a calf or lamb
montadito	a small toasted filled roll
morcilla	blood sausage, either solid or semi-liquid
morro	cheek, pork or lamb
mostaza	mustard
mosto	grape juice. Can also refer to a young wine, from 3 months old

N

naranja	orange
nata	sweet whipped cream
natillas	rich custard dessert
navajas	razor shells
nécora	small sea crab, sometimes called a velvet crab
nueces	walnuts

O

orejas	ears, usually of a pig
orujo	a fiery grape spirit, often brought to add to black coffee if the waiter likes you
ostras	oysters, also a common expression of dismay

P

paella	rice dish with saffron, seafood and/or meat
pan	bread
parrilla	grill; a *parrillada* is a mixed grill
pastel	cake/pastry

patatas	potatoes; often chips (*patatas fritas*, which confusingly can also refer to crisps); *bravas* are with a spicy tomato sauce	**plátano**	banana
		pluma	a cut of pork next to the loin
		pollo	chicken
		postre	dessert
pato	duck	**potaje**	a soup or stew
pavía	a crumbed and fried nugget of fish, usually *bacalao* or *merluza*.	**pringá**	a tasty paste of stewed meats usually eaten in a *montadito* and a traditional final tapa of the evening
pavo	turkey		
pechuga	breast (usually chicken)	**puerros**	leeks
perdiz	partridge	**pulpo**	octopus, particularly delicious *a la gallega*, boiled Galician style and garnished with olive oil, salt and paprika
pescado	fish		
pescaíto frito	Andalucían deep-fried fish and seafood		
pestiños	an Arabic-style confection of pastry and honey, traditionally eaten during Semana Santa		
		puntillitas	small squid, often served crumbed and deep fried
pez espada	swordfish; delicious; sometimes called *emperador*		
		Q/R	
		queso	cheese; *de cabra* (goat's), *oveja* (sheep's) or *vaca* (cow's). It comes fresh (*fresco*), medium (*semi-curado*) or strong (*curado*)
picadillo	a dish of spicy mincemeat		
picante	hot, ie spicy		
pichón	squab		
pijota	whiting	**rabo de buey/toro**	oxtail
pimienta	pepper		
pimientos	peppers; there are many kinds, *piquillos* are the trademark thin Basque red pepper; Padrón produces sweet green mini ones. A popular tapa is *pimientos aliñados* (marinated roasted peppers, often with onion, sometimes with tuna)	**ración**	a portion of food served in cafés and bars; check the size and order a half (*media*) if you want less
		rana	frog; *ancas de rana* is frogs' legs
		rape	monkfish/anglerfish
		raya	any of a variety of rays and skates
pincho	a small snack or grilled meat on a skewer (or *pinchito*)	**rebujito**	a weak mix of *manzanilla* and lemonade, consumed by the bucketload during Sevilla's Feria
pipas	sunflower seeds, a common snack		
		relleno/a	stuffed
pisto	a ratatouille-like vegetable concoction	**reserva, gran reserva, crianza**	terms relating to the age of wines; *gran reserva* is the oldest and finest, then *reserva* followed by *crianza*
plancha (a la)	grilled on a hot iron or fried in a pan without oil		

revuelto	scrambled eggs, usually with wild mushrooms (*setas*) or seafood; often a speciality
riñones	kidneys
rodaballo	turbot; pricey and delicious
romana (à la)	fried in batter
rosca	a large round dish, a cross between sandwich and pizza
rosquilla	doughnut

S

sal	salt
salchicha	sausage
salchichón	a salami-like sausage
salmón	salmon
salmonete	red mullet
salmorejo	a delicious thicker version of gazpacho, often garnished with egg and cured ham
salpicón	a seafood salad with plenty of onion and vinegar
salsa	sauce
San Jacobo	a steak cooked with ham and cheese
sandía	watermelon
sardinas	sardines, delicious grilled
sargo	white sea bream
seco	dry
secreto	a cut of pork loin
sepia	cuttlefish
serrano	see *jamón*
setas	wild mushrooms, often superb
sidra	cider
solomillo	beef or pork steak cut from the sirloin bone, deliciously fried in whisky and garlic in Sevilla (*solomillo al whisky*)
sopa	soup; *sopa castellana* is a broth with a fried egg, noodles, and bits of ham

T

tapa	a saucer-sized portion of bar food
tarta	tart or cake
té	tea
tenedor	fork
ternera	veal or young beef
tinto	red wine is *vino tinto*; a *tinto de verano* is mixed with lemonade and ice, a refreshing option
tocino	pork lard; *tocinillo de cielo* is a caramelized egg dessert
tomate	tomato
torrijas	a Semana Santa dessert, bread fried in milk and covered in honey and cinnamon
tortilla	a Spanish omelette, with potato, egg, olive oil and optional onion; *tortilla francesa* is a French omelette
tostada	toasted, also a toasted breakfast roll eaten with olive oil, tomato or paté
trucha	trout

U/V

uva	grape
vaso	glass
venado/ venao	venison
verduras	vegetables
vieiras	scallops, also called *veneras*
vino	wine; *blanco* is white, *rosado* or *clarete* is rosé, *tinto* is red

Z

zanahoria	carrot
zumo	fruit juice, usually bottled and pricey

Glossary of architectural terms

A

alcázar a Moorish fort

ambulatory a gallery round the chancel and behind the altar

apse vaulted square or rounded recess at the back of a church

archivolt decorative carving around the outer surface of an arch

art deco a style that evolved between the World Wars, based on geometric forms

artesonado ceiling ceiling of carved wooden panels with Islamic motifs popular throughout Spain in the 15th and 16th centuries

ayuntamiento a town hall

azulejo an ornamental ceramic tile

B

Baldacchino an ornate carved canopy above an altar or tomb

Baroque ornate architectural style of the 17th and 18th centuries

bodega a cellar where wine is kept or made; the term also refers to modern wineries and wine shops

buttress a pillar built into a wall to reinforce areas of greatest stress. A flying buttress is set away from the wall; a feature of Gothic architecture

C

capilla a chapel within a church or cathedral

capital the top of column, joining it to another section. Often highly decorated

castillo a castle or fort

catedral a cathedral, ie the seat of a bishop

chancel the area of a church which contains the main altar, usually at the eastern end

chapterhouse area reserved for Bible study in monastery or church

Churrigueresque a particularly ornate form of Spanish Baroque, named after the Churriguera brothers

colegiata a collegiate church, ie one ruled by a chapter of canons

conjunto histórico a tourist-board term referring to an area of historic buildings

convento a monastery or convent

coro the area enclosing the choirstalls, often central and completely closed off in Spanish churches

crossing the centre of a church, where the 'arms' of the cross join

E

ermita a hermitage or rural chapel

G

Gothic 13th-15th-century style formerly known as pointed style; distinguished externally by pinnacles and tracery around windows, Gothic architecture lays stress on the presence of light

H

hospital in pilgrimage terms, a place where pilgrims used to be able to rest, receive nourishment and receive medical attention

I
iglesia a church

L
lobed arch Moorish arch with depressions in the shape of simple arches

lonja a guildhall or fish market

M
mocárabes small concave spaces used as a decorative feature on Moorish ceilings and archways

modernista a particularly imaginative variant of art nouveau that came out of Catalonia; exemplified by Gaudí

monasterio a large monastery usually located in a rural area

monstrance a ceremonial container for displaying the host

Mozarabic the style of Christian artisans living under Moorish rule

mudéjar the work of Muslims living under Christian rule after the Reconquest, characterized by ornate brickwork

multifoil a type of Muslim-influenced arch with consecutive circular depressions

muralla a city wall

N
nave the main body of the church, a single or multiple passageway leading (usually) from the western end up to the crossing or high altar

neoclassical a reaction against the excesses of Spanish Baroque, this 18th- and 19th-century style saw clean lines and symmetry valued above all things

P
palacio a palace or large residence

patio an interior courtyard

pediment triangular section between top of collums and gables

pilaster pillar attached to the wall

Plateresque derived from *platero* (silversmith); used to describe a Spanish Renaissance stylecharacterized by finely carved decoration

R
reliquary a container to hold bones or remains of saints and other holy things

Renaissance Spanish Renaissance architecture began when classical motifs were used in combination with Gothic elements in the 16th century

retablo altarpiece or retable formed by many panels often rising to roof level; can be painted or sculptured

Romanesque (románico) style spread from France in the 11th and 12th centuries, characterized by barrel vaulting, rounded apses and semicircular arches

Romano Roman

S
sacristy (sacristía) part of church reserved for priests to prepare for services

soportales wooden or stone supports for the 1st floor of civic buildings, forming an arcade underneath

stucco (yesería) moulding mix consisting mainly of plaster; fundamental part of Moorish architecture

Notes

Index

Titles available in the Footprint *Focus* range

Latin America	UK RRP	US RRP
Bahia & Salvador	£7.99	$11.95
Brazilian Amazon	£7.99	$11.95
Brazilian Pantanal	£6.99	$9.95
Buenos Aires & Pampas	£7.99	$11.95
Cartagena & Caribbean Coast	£7.99	$11.95
Costa Rica	£8.99	$12.95
Cuzco, La Paz & Lake Titicaca	£8.99	$12.95
El Salvador	£5.99	$8.95
Guadalajara & Pacific Coast	£6.99	$9.95
Guatemala	£8.99	$12.95
Guyana, Guyane & Suriname	£5.99	$8.95
Havana	£6.99	$9.95
Honduras	£7.99	$11.95
Nicaragua	£7.99	$11.95
Northeast Argentina & Uruguay	£8.99	$12.95
Paraguay	£5.99	$8.95
Quito & Galápagos Islands	£7.99	$11.95
Recife & Northeast Brazil	£7.99	$11.95
Rio de Janeiro	£8.99	$12.95
São Paulo	£5.99	$8.95
Uruguay	£6.99	$9.95
Venezuela	£8.99	$12.95
Yucatán Peninsula	£6.99	$9.95

Asia	UK RRP	US RRP
Angkor Wat	£5.99	$8.95
Bali & Lombok	£8.99	$12.95
Chennai & Tamil Nadu	£8.99	$12.95
Chiang Mai & Northern Thailand	£7.99	$11.95
Goa	£6.99	$9.95
Gulf of Thailand	£8.99	$12.95
Hanoi & Northern Vietnam	£8.99	$12.95
Ho Chi Minh City & Mekong Delta	£7.99	$11.95
Java	£7.99	$11.95
Kerala	£7.99	$11.95
Kolkata & West Bengal	£5.99	$8.95
Mumbai & Gujarat	£8.99	$12.95

Africa & Middle East	UK RRP	US RRP
Beirut	£6.99	$9.95
Cairo & Nile Delta	£8.99	$12.95
Damascus	£5.99	$8.95
Durban & KwaZulu Natal	£8.99	$12.95
Fès & Northern Morocco	£8.99	$12.95
Jerusalem	£8.99	$12.95
Johannesburg & Kruger National Park	£7.99	$11.95
Kenya's Beaches	£8.99	$12.95
Kilimanjaro & Northern Tanzania	£8.99	$12.95
Luxor to Aswan	£8.99	$12.95
Nairobi & Rift Valley	£7.99	$11.95
Red Sea & Sinai	£7.99	$11.95
Zanzibar & Pemba	£7.99	$11.95

Europe	UK RRP	US RRP
Bilbao & Basque Region	£6.99	$9.95
Brittany West Coast	£7.99	$11.95
Cádiz & Costa de la Luz	£6.99	$9.95
Granada & Sierra Nevada	£6.99	$9.95
Languedoc: Carcassonne to Montpellier	£7.99	$11.95
Málaga	£5.99	$8.95
Marseille & Western Provence	£7.99	$11.95
Orkney & Shetland Islands	£5.99	$8.95
Santander & Picos de Europa	£7.99	$11.95
Sardinia: Alghero & the North	£7.99	$11.95
Sardinia: Cagliari & the South	£7.99	$11.95
Seville	£5.99	$8.95
Sicily: Palermo & the Northwest	£7.99	$11.95
Sicily: Catania & the Southeast	£7.99	$11.95
Siena & Southern Tuscany	£7.99	$11.95
Sorrento, Capri & Amalfi Coast	£6.99	$9.95
Skye & Outer Hebrides	£6.99	$9.95
Verona & Lake Garda	£7.99	$11.95

North America	UK RRP	US RRP
Vancouver & Rockies	£8.99	$12.95

Australasia	UK RRP	US RRP
Brisbane & Queensland	£8.99	$12.95
Perth	£7.99	$11.95

For the latest books, e-books and a wealth of travel information, visit us at:
www.footprinttravelguides.com.

footprinttravelguides.com

Join us on facebook for the latest travel news, product releases, offers and amazing competitions:
www.facebook.com/footprintbooks.